D0844773

The Logic of Pragmatism

H.S. THAYER

THE LOGIC

OF PRAGMATISM

AN EXAMINATION OF JOHN DEWEY'S LOGIC

GREENWOOD PRESS, PUBLISHERS
NEW YORK

ERRATA

Page vii For "Wendel T. Bush" read "Wendell T. Bush"

Page 36 line 12 for "physics say" read "physics says"

Page 55 line 4 for "criteria" read "criterion"

Page 73 line 14 for "rsults" read "results"

Page 74 line 15 for "...do not, in" read "...do not, in turn, jeopardize the other features of Dewey's theory. In the"

Page 80 line 3 from bottom, for "is animism at" read "is animism at the expense of subjectivism in psychology"

Page 81 line 9 for "criteria" read "criterion"

Page 86 line 6 for "stoge" read "stage"

Page 86 line 12 delete entire and read "tlement takes place. 'The final judgment arrived at' "

Page 124 line 15 for "falsehood from" read "falsehood of"

Page 124 line 26 for "tions as the" read "tion as the"

Page 138 bottom line for "to the end" read "of the end"

Page 144 line 4 for "inquiry we" read "inquiry in" and delete line 5 entire.

Page 148 line 10 for "time is" read "time it"

Page 155 line 7 for "perhaps on" read "perhaps an"

Page 158 line 21 delete the hyphen after "*every*"

Page 180 lines 14-15 for "reckin" read "reckon"

Page 182 line 25 for "transform a" read "transform or"

Page 183 line 13 for "size and" read "size an"

Page 185 line 3 from bottom for "in view what" read "in view of what"

Page 190 line 22 for "casual property" read "causal property"

CONTENTS

Contents

ACKNOWLEDGMENTS

I WISH to express my deep obligation to Professor Ernest Nagel who read the manuscript of this work; his insights and valuable suggestions concerning the themes as developed in this essay served as a constant source of inspiration. His insistence on clarity, rigor, and on informed and responsible inquiry in philosophy, as in the sciences, has always made philosophic discussion with him both exciting and profitable. I am also greatly indebted to Professors Irwin Edman and James Gutmann; their friendship and encouragement has meant much to more than one beginner in philosophy. I want to thank Professor Justus Buchler for reading the manuscript and offering a number of important suggestions. To Professors John Herman Randall, Jr., Herbert W. Schneider, Horace L. Friess and Dr. John C. Cooley I am grateful for criticism, instruction and advice.

I also want to acknowledge my gratitude to Mrs. Wendel T. Bush who has established the Wendel T. Bush Fellowship in philosophy at Columbia University. Without the aid of this Fellowship I do not think the following study could have been written. My thanks to Frederick B. Boyden for his assistance in the preparation of the typscript as well as for his helpful criticism of the book.

To Henry Holt and Company I am especially indebted for gracious permission to quote frequently and occasionally at length from Dewey's *Logic*: *The Theory of Inquiry*. I also want to thank each and all of the publishers of the books and periodicals mentioned in part 1 of the Bibliography for granting me permission to quote from these works.

H. S. T.

New York, 1950.

INTRODUCTION

HERE IS a critical essay on John Dewey's philosophy. To many, dubious about the leading ideas of this philosopher, it will in two respects not seem critical enough. It is not intended as a dismissal or belittling of the positive contributions of a major philosophy, nor does it deal with anything but certain difficulties in the logic of Dewey's logical theory. It will thus doubtless seem inadequate to devotees who find many of Dewey's ideas ignored in these pages, and who may think that undue importance has been given to the particular themes discussed and criticized.

If the subject of this examination may be described as consisting of matters of logic it must be remembered that "logic" in Dewey's terminology covers more than the construction and analysis of deductive and formalized systems. The scope of logic, according to Dewey, may be described in a general sense as the articulation and explicit formulation of the controlling instrumentalities and operations that function when problems are being inquired into and warranted solutions are arrived at. The theory of inquiry is a descriptive explanation of what happens when problems are investigated and solved logically or methodically and deliberately, with respect to the means taken to reach solutions. The pattern of inquiry, as a mediating process bringing about a settled or solved situation in an initially unsettled one, exhibits certain characteristic phases as certain operations are performed. What usually passes for logic and scientific method are not contrasted as two kinds of rational techniques for dealing with certain kinds of problems, but are incorperated as designating procedural and material means within the general movement of inquiry.

It is this theory of inquiry which is dealt with critically and in some detail in chapter three; this examination constitutes the major portion of the pages to follow. However, before turning directly to the particular problems occupying us in the pages to come, I have tried to introduce the general topic *inquiry,* by briefly describing the natural world in which inquiries are found to take place. The themes of experience and nature, which appear as fundamental notions in Dewey's philosophy, are set down here and serve to place the scrutiny of inquiry in its proper setting with respect to the materials and forces which sustain inquiries. Experience and nature are the parents of inquiry and though it function as the instrument of human survival it is nonetheless by them that the offspring is shaped and taught the lessons for which it was brought into being. These preliminary matters are discussed in chapter one.

Next, in chapter two, the activities making up the distinguishing features of common sense and science are dealt with and attention is drawn to the role played by the function of inquiry in each. The pattern of inquiry is traced and certain fundamental notions raised by Dewey's account of these stages or phases of inquiry are discussed. Chapter three consists of an analysis of three topics having to do with the initial, intermediate and final stages in the pattern of inquiry as Dewey has formulated it. I have criticised what I take to be important shortcomings in

Dewey's treatment of these issues and, in the light of the difficulties raised, have attempted to suggest how these problems may be satisfactorily overcome. As I have provided, in the first few pages of chapter three, an introduction to the topics to be considered there, I will avoid repetition by saying nothing more about these matters for the present.

The method which I have tried to employ throughout this essay may be stated roughly as proceeding in the following order: first, clarification of the meaning of that particular point or feature of Dewey's thought which we may be occupied with; secondly, supposing the idea clarified, the evidence for it is considered; finally, depending on the outcome of these preliminary steps, an alternative or revised formulation of the original point may be in order and, if so, will be suggested. Dewey's writings are not always easily understood and consequently determination of *the* meaning (i.e., Dewey's meaning) of a statement may force one to consider several possibilities each one of which might appear to various readers to be the real meaning of the point in question. If an analysis of such an issue is to be adequate it must cover each of these possibilities; this often takes time and space and may tax the readers patience, but I know of no short-cuts by which sound conclusions can be arrived at in such matters as these.

It should be said that historical questions as to the origins of certain of Dewey's views are not directly relevant to the present study—except insofar as they aid in understanding certain of the ideas discussed. For example, there are important historical reasons which explain why Dewey holds that propositions do not possess the properties of truth or falsehood. I have not tried to give an account of these and have only mentioned them in passing. The striking feature of this view, and of particular concern to the present study, is its unfortunate consequences for Dewey's own logical theory. Most surprising, perhaps, are the consequences for Dewey's well-known theory of truth or warranted assertion. For, as I have tried to show, if warranted assertions assert something about propositions, namely that they are true or that they are false, but propositions are by definition neither true nor false, then every warranted assertion must be false. Every warranted assertion must be false since (for the reasons given in section D) no warranted assertion could be true if it asserted something to be the case concerning propositions which, by definition or prior agreement, is not the case at all.

The importance of Dewey's contributions to philosophy needs no recounting here. The significance of his thought and its consequent influence on other areas of learning is evident to anyone not completely blind to the trends and characteristics of present day thinking. The fact that Dewey has effected so fundamental a reconstruction in philosophy that hardly any contemporary school of doctrine has been left without his influence may be one reason why his own line of thought has been characterized variously as materialism, idealism, overly intellectual, anti-intellectual, all practice, all theory, etc.

Dewey's own outlook on existing ideas has been for the most part critical; and no one has insisted more persuasively than he that philosophy take a lesson in responsibility from the sciences as well as every day affairs where the appreciation of controlled thinking and its consequences is a dominant and working ideal. It is in this same spirit that I have attempted to pursue the themes in the following pages.

CHAPTER I.

THE LIVE CREATURE, NATURE AND EXPERIENCE

THAT LIFE seeks to sustain itself is a fact exhibited in the behavior of all living creatures. For the world is not wholly propitious to living things and the careers of animals are precarious and uneven, marked with the loom and thrust of unforseen elements threatening the continuance of life. To early experience the world may seem an onslaught of impressions and movements. None-the-less even in such swarming and seemingly disordered passages of experience there appears, on the part of the creature involved, a prehensile and inarticulate movement for those goods, located in the immediate, which promise sustenance. Such behavior may be marked by success, in the transition from one immediate situation to the next, or by failure and death. And in early experience, as it appears with simple or undeveloped organisms, life is largely a matter of chance and circumstance; since whatever activity of preservation is manifested, it is unplanned, sporadic, and absent of past and future considerations, pinning all on the immediate for salvation.

Intelligence, as it appears in human beings, distinguishing men from animals and early experience, is a radical

13

factor in reducing (though not eliminating) the chance-like and precarious nature of existence. The organs of intelligence, like all natural organs, have a long antecedent natural history and animal ancestry. Yet their appearance and function did not of itself render the world more friendly to human life. They did make possible a retention of former struggles and experiences, an ability to bring this store of information to bear on immediate situations, and to calculate or anticipate a specific outcome. It would be a mistake, however, to think that with the arrival of intelligence men no longer shared with all life those same vital needs; or that intelligence was itself something separate and apart from the active struggle for survival.

It is only the sophistication of relatively secure and modern society which leads us to overlook the precarious character of life. But the fact has not changed, it has only been obscured. Reason, when it forgets its function as the vital organ in ordering and securing the goods of life, and forgets its place in nature as well as its own history, borders on madness. For to deny the world and the vocation of living—if it could be done seriously—would exhibit the strange spectacle of a mind, which, in refusing to recognize the very forces that nourish it, had severed itself from the roots of sanity.

This is not to neglect the fact that, in disillusionment and disappointment with the rough and often fearful struggle for life, some single minds may be led to soliloquize of other and better worlds—worlds indeed not located in regions accessible to ordinary experience and natural knowledge, but to whose more favorable climates loyalties may be pledged and citizenship desired. But such a turn of thought, for all its imaginative force, cannot escape reflecting its natural origins, and can claim to be reasonable only insofar as it is considerate of and efficacious in shaping and directing human life in this world. The legitimate hope then, and indeed our only hope, for survival and well-being in a world half wild and half alien to human interests, will be a faith in human intelligence: in its capacity to organize and control those features and materials of the world as can be brought into accord with what is humanly needed, prized, and desired.

The above considerations and remarks may seem the merest commonplaces and of trivial import. Yet they have important implications for philosophy in general and John Dewey's philosophy in particular.* By way of this latter implication, three words, prominent in what has been said above, designate three crucial themes in Dewey's philosophy. These are: *nature, experience,* and *intelligence.* We shall be concerned in this essay with that range of thought characterized by the word *intelligence.* That is, specifically, with Dewey's theory of inquiry. But so significant to an adequate discussion of this part of Dewey's philosophy are the themes of nature and experience that we must give them some prior attention. For it is within the setting of nature and experience that human intelligence is nourished and discovers its vocation and function.

1.

NATURE

NATURE, Dewey writes, is an affair of affairs.[1] That is to say, nature is a kind of moving and all-inclusive history of a vast multitude of histories. Every natural thing has its own history, its own quality as shaped in the interactive sequential continuum of all things. That particular history and quality of a thing may change as its linkage, its interaction with other things, may change; yet as a thing it has a history, however multifarious and marked by change that history may be. One event, or thing may unite in a continuous interaction with some other thing in such a way that their separate histories and careers may be said to impinge and interlock; there is a continuity established between them. That union may continue in time to establish a common history of what was formerly two separate and distinct histories, or some other occurrence and transaction may break it off. One event in the relation becomes separated from the other, marking and end to the common history. Each thing, carrying something of the former situation with it, is sent into a new and different situation.

Insofar as we may wish to call the interlocking of things and histories into a structure and completed affair, having its own history, and quality, a *separate* history, we may speak of beginnings and endings of natural histories. For the beginning and ending of a history, or an affair, will be that span of time in which an event or events are moved and brought into some stable, continuous equilibrium: a situation having its own uniquely designated character and quality. That particular kind of a situation, whether it be the span of a man's life, the passage of a day or a season, the roll of a wave or the flight of a bird, may be properly said to have a beginning and an ending. And the ending of one situation or history, Dewey stresses, is the beginning of another.[2]

Each separate thing in nature, each event, then, has a history, and that history is itself a history of changes; of beginnings and endings, of interactions and continuities. And just as each thing is an ongoing history of histories, so nature is in the most inclusive sense the vast spectacle and setting, the on-going history of all histories. Running through all nature, and effecting the function of every natural activity are two principles: those of continuity and interaction. As one commentator on Dewey has put it: "The Nature within which we live is an ongoing history of ongoing histories. When an event is connected with another event as cause-effect, that connection is the exemplification of the continuity between them. But that connection of continuity is the funded history of interaction and the effect is the funded consequence, the terminal phase of the inclusive history of cause-effect. 'The two principles of continuity and interaction are not separate from each other. They intercept and unite. They are so to speak, the longitudinal and lateral aspects' of every history, of every situation, of every sequential order, of every connection of cause-effect." [3]

The same writer speaks of Dewey's meaning of the term *nature* in this way: "Nature is an inclusive history of multitudinous ongoing histories, the comprehensive interactive continuum consequent upon the interactivities of an indefinite number of general kinds." [4]

In addition to the principles of continuity and interaction there appears, in Dewey's conception of nature, another significant feature crucial to human life and experience. A feature which, in classical philosophy, went by the title of permanence and change. Dewey writes: "There is in nature, even below the level of life, something more than mere flux and change. Form is arrived at whenever a stable, even though moving, equilibrium is reached. Changes interlock and sustain one another. Wherever there is coherence there is endurance. Order is not imposed from without but is made out of the relations of harmonious interactions that energies bear to one another. Because it is active (not anything static because foreign to what goes on) order itself develops. It comes to include within its balanced movement a greater variety of changes.

"Order cannot but be admirable in a world constantly threatened with disorder—in a world where living creatures can go on living only by taking advantage of whatever order exists about them, incorporating it into themselves. In a world like ours, every living creature that attains sensibility welcomes order. For only when an organism shares in the ordered relations of its environment does it secure the stability essential to living."[5]

In this "taking advantage of whatever order exists" (and our lives depend upon it) human intelligence finds its role. When intelligence or inquiry, drawing on the only materials and source available to it, human experience, becomes shared (i.e., when its techniques become institutionalized and social and work within a common fund of human experience) science appears on the human scene.

We are thus led back to earlier considerations. Human life, taking place in nature, in striving to sustain itself, finds some elements in its environment stable and secure; others transitory and indifferent, even hostile to life. Intelligence is the human weapon by which the essentials of life are carved from the world. But the exercise of intelligence does not take place in a vacuum: intelligence works with the materials and by the means of human experience. It seizes on, organizes, directs and transforms those parts of experience which are relevant to the securing of some deliberate, planned outcome—some consummatory end-in-view.

An exposition, however brief and inadequate it might be, of Dewey's conception of nature, must, if it is to be in any sense complete, lead into and include considerations of experience. For included as a natural affair in nature is the way nature is to be known. If the natural prerequisite for knowing anything is experience, in knowing this much, intelligence has learned its first lesson. And the theme of experience is certainly most central to all of Dewey's philosophy. It is, therefore, appropriate in a discussion of his theory of inquiry, to begin where Dewey maintains all intelligence must begin: with experience.

2.

EXPERIENCE

EXPERIENCE is an old word in philosophy and as such is loaded with certain traditional affiliations and associations. Add to this fact that in various writings on various subjects Dewey is concerned to emphasize different aspects of what he understands experience to be, and the resulting confusion and numerous discussions concerning Dewey's meaning of experience may be partially explained. I will not be concerned with criticising or attempting to justify the choice of the word 'experience' to designate those areas and occurrences in nature which Dewey means to point out and emphasize in employing that word. Rather an attempt shall be made to give as clear and sufficient account of what Dewey intends to denote by 'experience' as is possible, in order to illumine and set the stage for the subsequent discussion of inquiry (called by Dewey the method of experience) in common sense and science.

Having stated the matter this way it will be seen that our task is not altogether an easy one. For it is apparent that Dewey, in departing from the more narrow usage of an older empiricism, gives the idea of experience a much more fundamental and significant status. Fundamental ideas, especially when born from original minds, are apt to appear strange and confusing to unrehearsed eyes. We may wonder, and that wonder may be illustrated in the present case, by the following seemingly different intentions Dewey gives to the word 'experience.'

(1) ..."experience is *of* as well as *in* nature. It is not experience which is experienced but nature—stones, plants, animals, diseases, health, temperature, and so on. Things interacting in certain ways *are* experience; they are what is experienced. Linked in certain ways with another natural object—the human organism—they are *how* things are experienced as well."[6]

(2) "Experience occurs continuously, because the inter-action of live creature and environing conditions is involved in the very process of living.....Often times, however, the experience had is inchoate. Things are experienced but not in such a way that they are composed into an experience——In contrast with such experience, we have *an* experience when the material experienced runs its course to fullfillment. Then and then only is it integrated within and demarcated in the general stream of experience from other experiences.....It is *an* experience."[7]

(3) "Experience becomes an affair primarily of doing ....The organism acts in accordance with its own structure, simple or complex, upon its surroundings. As a consequence the changes produced in the environment react upon the organism and its activities....This close connection between doing and suffering or undergoing forms what we call experience."[8] "...the interaction of organism and environment, resulting in some adaption which secures utilization of the latter, is the primary fact, the basic category."[9]

Here, then, we have three statements of what Dewey means by 'experience.' In the latter two we find support for the usual assertion that 'experience', for Dewey, denotes the interaction of a living organism with its environment.

But implicit in these quotations and explicit in the context of the discussions from which they have been taken are two fundamental considerations. First, to say that 'experience' designates the interaction of an organism with its environment is intended to convey more than the mere fact that interaction occurs. To speak of interaction is to point out a significant but skeletal fact; experience includes not only the bone, but the life blood and flesh of this interaction. Experience is more than the abstract claim that there *is* such interaction; it makes this claim, but stresses all the on-going qualities, changes, and features which flow as consequences from it; consequences of vital significance to living and reflection.[10]

The second important matter to be noted in the above quotations is the difference drawn in the degrees of significance of experience. In the second quotation Dewey clearly distinguishes *an* experience from a more general and primitive flow of experience. There are other passages in Dewey's writings where he marks this difference in terms of "primary" or "crude" and the "refined objects of reflection." He writes: "The consideration of method may suitably begin with the contrast between gross, macroscopic, crude subject matters in primary experience and the refined, derived objects of reflection. The distinction is one between what is experienced as the result of a minimum of incidental reflection and what is experienced in consequence of continued and regulated reflective inquiry." [11] Any organism, then, as long as it can be said to be living, is one part of a process of interaction with the environment. For "life denotes a function, a comprehensive activity, in which organism and environment are included."[12] The function of intelligence, like the organs of digestion, can be said to be interacting with an environment, just as much as the more obvious movement of a limb—be it an arm or wing or fin—works with, mediates, and visibly transforms areas and part of the environment.

Experience is thus ongoing; it is an affair in nature. It has its own qualitative dimensions and structure, its own histories, its continuity of beginnings and endings: those organized phases where, within the wide flow of experience, there is an integrating and arresting of elements and form has been achieved.

The significance of Dewey's conception of experience as providing both the materials and methods of inquiry (especially as exhibited in the natural sciences) cannot be overemphasized. It is quite obvious that experience, as an ongoing affair between live creatures and their environments, provides the only access and means to what can be known about nature. Man experiences nature, he develops organs and techniques for refining that experience, making it richer, more penetrating, and significant. He draws on a fund of former experiences of his own and indirectly of others, giving depth of meaning to the present. In all, the philosophic problem is how experience is to be interpreted. Dewey's contribution stands as a landmark in the history of thought. For here philisophies may first differ and part company; each draws its own map of the territory it takes to be the world and discovers for itself where and how in the episode of things as it traces them the course of knowing and knowns is to be made articulate.

That experience is the necessary condition for knowing, is true enough, if this means that whatever thing may swim through the moving universe, if it can be known at all, must reveal itself in human experience.

3.

EXPERIENCE AS METHOD:
INTERACTION AND TRANSACTION

THE most obvious and fundamental things are easily missed and often require painstaking study before being detected; all their apparent bulk suddenly betraying them to have been resting so perpetually before our eyes that vision was blind to them. Familiarity also breeds inattention. Experience, when it is finally recognized for what it is, when saluted and discerned by reflective minds, has much to teach to animals bent on knowing the contents of their natural surroundings. Chief among the riches experience has to offer, is the disclosure of a way to further riches in nature; For experience provides its own method, a conduit leading reason to the things it prizes and is intent on securing.

"Experience," writes Dewey, "presents itself as the method, and the only method, for getting at nature, penetrating its secrets, and wherein nature empirically disclosed (by the use of empirical method in natural science) deepens, enriches and directs the further development of experience." Here is the emphasis on experience as method, and Dewey continues: "In the natural sciences there is a union of experience and nature which is not greeted as a monstrosity; on the contrary, the inquirer must use empirical method if his findings are to be treated as genuinely scientific. The investigator assumes as a matter of course that experience, controlled in specifiable ways, is the avenue that leads to the facts and laws of nature. He uses reason and calculation freely; he could not get along without them. But he sees to it that ventures of this theoretical sort start from and terminate in directly experienced subject-matter."[13]

Experience, in providing the only access to nature, provides the means and techniques by which nature and things-to-be-known are explored and revealed. Experience is the started point of all inquiries; for, in view of what has been said about experience, where else and with what but the materials of experience could inquiry conceivably begin? And insofar as inquiry is controlled and directed, it is taking into account and employing experience as the method for dealing with nature. When an inquiry comes to a close, however abstract it has been or distantly it has wandered from the present, its conclusions are matters of direct experience. These observations are liable to be misunderstood: the emphasis on experience, and on direct or immediate experience as the outcome of inquiries, has led critics to ask Dewey, how events, of which we find evidence, occurring millions of years ago can be explained in terms of experience. The implication being that these events ought rightly to be considered as outside any consideration of experience. But according to Dewey's account of experience, any event or occurrence which can be said to be outside, or beyond experience, is unknown—it cannot rightly be talked about. What then about past events; can I know through experience, something about occurrences that took place before I, or in some cases the whole race, was born? The question is an important one and I quote at some length Dewey's answer to it.

The beginning or starting point of any speculation about the past or future must, he says, take place among the materials of present experience. "Visiting a natural history museum, one beholds a mass of rock and, reading a label, finds that it comes from a tree that grew, so it is affirmed, five million years ago. The geologist did not leap from a thing he can see and touch to some event in bygone ages; he collected this observed thing with many others, of different kinds, found all over the globe; the results of his comparisons he then compared with data of other experiences, say, the astronomers. *He translates, that is, observed coexistences into non-observed, inferred sequences.* Finally he dates his object, placing it in an order of events. By the same sort of method he predicts that at certain places some things not yet experienced will be observed, and then he takes pains to bring them within the scope of experience."[14] The scientist may, if his conscience demands and materials allow it, try to re-create in experiment those conditions which he infers once existed, in order to observe directly the consequences which he has inferred took place under similar conditions.

The emphasis that Dewey puts on the directly experienced, as both the starting point and terminus of inquiry, should not therefore, be taken to mean that he regards only the immediate to be real.[15] The existence of a past and the coming of a future are not denied; but these existences are known only to the extent that the materials of present experience can be worked and wrung of such evidential data as to warrant inference concerning past events and histories, as well as predictions of future events.

Experience as method involves a distinction between experience and experiencing. We are thus led directly to certain more technical writings where Dewey has exhibited the distinction and shown its significance to be very clear.

We have seen that Dewey, in using the word experience, means more than a formal recognition that organisms interact with their environment. For that interaction does occur would seem to be a patent fact which very little re-flection and observation would make sufficiently evident. But important consequences flow from this fact, and Dewey's conception of experience is designed to take them into account. Experience is consequently to be taken as a context; not a state of mind or immediate contents of consciousness. Nor is it a kind of flowing medium between "mind" at one end, and "objects of mind" attached at the other. Experience as a context rather includes both knower and known; a context with a qualitative milieu of differences; the histories making up the factors involved in that context; what is done and suffered by those factors—the changes taking place as each participates with the other, the consequences as action goes on, etc.

Perhaps in order to emphasize these considerations Dewey has, in certain recent writings, employed the word 'trans-action.' Use of 'transaction' draws attention "to the fact that human life itself, both severally and collectively, consists of transactions in which human beings partake together with non-human things of the milieu along with other human beings, so that without this togetherness of human and non-human partakers we could not even stay alive, to say nothing of accomplishing anything. From birth to death every human being is a *Party,* so that neither he nor anything done or suffered can possibly be understood when it is separated from the fact of parti-cipation in an extensive body of transactions—to which a given human being may contribute and which he modi-fies, but only in virtue of being a partaker in them."[16]

The methodological import of the use of this notion of transaction is great, and deserves careful analysis on its own account. For Dewey (writing in collaboration with Mr. Arthur F. Bently) has claimed that the revolution in modern physical theory is to be regarded as a change from interactional to transactional techniques of explanation an inquiry.[17] Since I am concerned with rounding out Dewey's account of experience, I will not enter into a detailed discussion of these recent writings. But one may say in passing, that interactional explanations seem to be those which, singling out and isolating from some context certain carefully connected elements, deal with them as isolated systems, i.e., as independent of other systems and contexts. And transactional explanations are those which, in locating some feature within a context for analysis, include the relations that particular feature has to the context as a necessary part of the explanation. What needs to be noted here, and seems to rest at the heart of this notion of transaction, is the insistence that inquiry or analysis not commit the error of over-emphasizing and isolating one feature in the context of experience to the extent that some dualism may be the result: that is, in *distinguishing* knower from known, not to go on and make one a subject, the other an object, from which the leap to subjective-objective, mind-matter, internal and external worlds, etc., is accomplished. Dewey is constantly on guard against this direction of analysis, which so often results in perplexing and paradoxical issues going under the heading of "problems of knowledge."

Nowhere have these dualisms had more damaging influence than in the analysis of human conduct and behavior. It was against just such malicious turns of analysis and doctrinaire accretions, that Dewey in an important paper on "Conduct and Experience" in 1933, seems to have first deliberately used the word 'transaction' with the force and intention he now gives it. In this somewhat technical paper his conception of experience and its methodological significance also appears with clarity and force. Throughout his entire discussion of behavior and the way behavior is to be studied, the theme of experience is implicitly present. Speaking specifically of the idea of stimulus and response—an idea which has often occasioned the severing and separation of individual from environment, and regarded behavior as the mere additive sum of 'external stimuli'—Dewey writes: "There is something in the *context* of experiment which goes beyond the stimuli and responses directly found within it. There is, for example, the *problem* which the experimenter has set and his deliberate arrangement of apparatus and selection of conditions with a view to disclosure of facts that bear upon it. There is also an *intent* on the part of the subject." And all these factors, Dewey continues, "call attention to a definite characteristic of behavior, namely, that it is not exhausted in the immediate stimuli-response features of the experimentation. From the standpoint of behavior itself, the traits in question take us beyond the isolated act of the subject into a content that has a temporal spread."[18] These acts being discussed came out of one situation and move into another; they have continuity. "Their whole scientific point is lost unless they are placed as one phase in this contextual behavior."[19]

Behavior is thus not a serial line of successive movements. It can be observed and dissected into discrete acts, as analysis may demand, "but no act can be understood apart from the series to which it belongs."[20]

Those remarks place our understanding of stimulus in a new light. For within the active context and function of behavior "something, not yet a stimulus, breaks in upon an activity already going on and *becomes* a stimulus in virtue of the relations it sustains to what is going on in this continuing activity." No external activity is a stimulus in itself, no matter how such a motion or change may seem to break in upon behavior. For the particular force of the stimulus, its character and quality, its abrupt effect on the organism, is determined by "what the organism is already doing in interaction with a particular environment."[21] A crash of thunder will have different effects on an organism, depending on what that organism has been doing before the stimulus is received. We may have expected the din, or it may have come as a shocking and startling interruption to a train of behavior. In each case the efficacious character of the stimulus is determined by, and depends upon, the kind of behavior that has been going on.[22]

Putting some of the consequences of these remarks in more general form, Dewey says: "No organism is so isolated that it can be understood apart from the environment in which it lives. Sensory receptors and muscular effectors, the eye and the hand, have their existence as well as their meaning because of connections with an outer environment.....The structure of whatever is had by way of immediate qualitative presences is found in the recurrent modes of interaction taking place between what we term organism, on the one side, and environment on the other. *This interaction is the primary fact and it constitutes a trans-action.* Only by analysis and selective abstraction can we differentiate the actual occurrence into two factors, one called organism and the other, environment." [23]

Behavior then, taking place in the continuum, the temporal continuity and spread of interactions, of experience, is transactional in form. The notion of independent entities, of stimuli and responses as isolated features and closed serial spurts of action, of organism and environment as separate halves and independent orbits of action, are eliminated in Dewey's account of behavior as misleading and scientifically unwarranted.

I mentioned some time back Dewey's insistence on distinguishing experience from experiencing. He makes some illuminating remarks on this matter in this same paper. Experience as a subject-matter is distinguished from experiencing, or the way humans get at a subject matter. Yet the two are intimately related since experiencing is itself a fact of experience. "The psychologist" he writes, "is concerned exclusively with experiencing, with detection, analysis, and description of its different modes. Experienc*ing* has no existence apart from subject-matter experienced; we perceive objects, veridical or illusory, not percepts; we remember events and not memories; we think topics and subjects, not thoughts; we love persons, not loves; and so on. . .Experiencing is not itself an immediate subject-matter; it is not experienced as a complete and self-sufficient event. But everything experienced is in part made what it is because there enteres into it a way of experiencing something; not a way of experiencing *it,* which would be self contradictory, but a way of experiencing something other than itself. No complete account of what is experienced, then, can be given until we know *how* it is experienced or the mode of experiencing that entered into its formulation."[24]

In considering experience as method, this distinction between experience and experiencing is a crucial one. It is illustrated by taking, for example, our experience of some object, say a tree. "The tree, when it is perceived, is experienced in one way; when remembered, reflected upon, or admired for its beauty, it is experienced in other ways. By a certain figure of speech we may call it an experience, meaning that it is experienced, but we cannot by any figure of speech call it an experiencing. Nevertheless, the tree *as* experienced lends itself to a different type of analysis than that which is appropriate to the tree as a botanical object. We can first discriminate various ways of experiencing it, namely, perceptually, reflectively, emotionally, practically—as a lumberman might look at it—and then we can attempt to analyze scientifically the structure and mechanism of the various acts involved."[25]

More generally then, we can say experience gives access to that which can be known as well as the method of knowing. That method, says Dewey, is one which has respect for experience.

And we may conclude by observing that this method itself may be the subject-matter for study and investigation. Just as a carpenter, when the need is felt, may turn from the house to be built, to examining his tools and perhaps organizing and adjusting these instruments with the hope of making them more efficient and efficacious. Much of modern philosophy has been doing the same; attention being on man the knower and on the instruments of knowing, rather than the world to be known and the ends to which knowing and its instruments are addressed. Dewey has been particularly concerned to indicate the practical and theoretical significance that consideration of experience will have for modern thought, preoccupied as it is with matters of methodology. He has worked out what he takes to be *the* method of experience, the empirical method; and he has discussed some of those intricacies and problems of logic and empirical procedure which have consequently presented themselves. It is to this method and to some of these related issues that we now must turn.

CHAPTER II.

COMMON SENSE, SCIENCE AND THE PATTERN OF INQUIRY

NATURE, taken discursively, is the name for a class: a class having as its members the procession of events and histories that men have variously called the universe, reality, or world, seas and sky and all that in them are. Given its material designation the term is dramatic. It points to a seething and seminal context: not a formless flux but a moving mechanism and network of events, histories and the recipient of their manifold futures. This is the sentient womb of things—as well as of life, and of human life in all of its significance—apprehended at best only dimly. Whatever urges this dramatic setting may prompt in human beings, they are rendered articulate and best celebrated in works of art.

Experience is located in this reticulate and interacting movement of events; experiencing animals are thereby able to awaken what powers of reason they may have from the slumber of non-being. They discover a world about them. If the roots and tendrils of reason are lodged in the restless seed-ground of experience and nature, its flowering is in human inquiry. Inquiry is reason come of age. The progress of reason consists in an ever recurring

32

attention to origins, means and ends; <u>its method is</u> <u>genetic-functional</u>. The ambition of intelligence is to know the materials and forces from which it was born and nourished, in order to know what ends and futures its existence can best strive to realize. In giving birth to reason nature, as it were, having nothing else to turn to, provides part of itself as its own interlocutor. So, at least, one is tempted to sum up metaphorically, the previous discussion of Dewey's conception of the place of reason in experience and nature.

If life is, as we have been saying, a practical predicament, and reason is a candid instrument of human survival, when duly chastised by these exigencies, reason is efficacious. Reason is discovered and displayed when, regardless of the particular locale and quality of some subject of concern to an individual, a response is forthcoming which deliberately mediates and works the situation into one having those qualities and characteristics initially forseen, planned and hoped for by the responding individual. When behavior of this sort is normally functioning, it exhibits a general pattern, a routine is gone through; responses are adjusted not only according to what may be presented in one given situation, but also according to certain <u>habits</u> which are the general by-products and retained outcomes, carried over from former adjustments, from what was learned and experienced in previous situations. This kind of behavior is, to some extent at least, calculated or controlled and proceeds by certain guiding principles. It has, in popular expression, "logic" to it.

Whatever the particular problem may be to which intelligence is addressed, in action intelligence or inquiry goes through certain procedures and articulates kinds of operations. Or, better, inquiry has pattern and form; it moves in certain stages, having functional phases which betray and characterize, as points on a map, its over-all process, from start to conclusion. This pattern of inquiry is the same, and occurs, Dewey maintains, regardless of whether an inquiry be of the most mundane and passing, or of the most advanced and scientific sort. That is, the general pattern of inquiry remains largely the same, though the status and occurrence of inquiries may be as assorted and miscellaneous as the particular objects initiating them. An inquiry in a science, though far more refined and controlled, is no different in its over-all characteristic (*as* an inquiry) than the common sense and practical inquiries of every day life. Common sense and science are thus not set apart from each other as radically different enterprises, each employing different methods of thinking.

This is a significant line of thought for a philosophy which wishes to formulate and explain scientific procedure as growing out of, rather than pursuing a course against, common sense disciplines and the practical affairs of living. For there is a familiar and influential argument running directly opposite to this one. Since it may serve, by way of contrast, to illustrate Dewey's own view and some of the problems Dewey has been particularly concerned with, let us briefly trace certain of the main themes of this other and, I suspect, more influential view.

1.
COMMON SENSE AND SCIENCE

SCIENTIFIC procedure is often severely distinguished from what goes by the name of common sense. And when that distinction is made in much of the current philosophical literature, common sense comes out the worse for it. For common sense is first taken to be a body of beliefs which are common to all men or very widely shared. These beliefs emerge from a residue of the most elementary kind of experience; they are not products of method or deliberation. They are uncritical and have their origin in no special human exertion, but are merely the products of living. The belief that spring will follow winter, or that water will quench thirst, are examples of this untutored experience. Early life is sustained by just such knowledge as this, and later men and communities continue to draw on this fund of practical and native beliefs in the conduct of daily existence. As such, these beliefs constitute the roots of conduct and living; however absently, we nonetheless maintain them and continue to hold most of them even when the most sophisticated analysis persuades us that it is a mistake to do so. For in spite of their crude and primitive status on the scale of knowledge, they are part of the necessary conditions for daily life and the survival of intelligence.

Because they are uncritically arrived at, common sense beliefs are in good part vague and often inconsistent. Water quenches thirst *in general,* but there are circumstances (e.g., in the case of certain diseases) where it doesn't. A common sense maxim bids us look before we leap, while another advises that he who hesitates is lost.

To a body of beliefs making no claim to systematization or consistency, these objections may not appear serious or relevant. For there is an implicit supposition that these beliefs are relative to certain situations: their applicability is not universal. Hence the success and utility of one belief employed rather than another, will depend on the perspicuity and wit of the individual in determining whether or not an accepted piece of common sense knowledge is applicable to some given situation.

Here the familiar argument against common sense finds momentum. In having an essentially uncritical origin and in failing to specify the range and applicability of its sorted beliefs, as well as in being inconsistent when considered as a body of beliefs as such, common sense has been called "cocksure, vague, and self-contradictory." [1] It is identified and characterized as *naive realism*. We believe, we are told, that the table we may be looking at is a hard, colored, material object. But, we are immediately assured, "physics say that the table or chair is 'really' an incredibly vast system of electrons and protons in rapid motion, with empty space in between." And we are further told "that light-waves start from the electrons and protons (or, more probably, are reflected by them from a source of light), reach the eye, have a series of effects upon the rods and cones, the optic nerve, and the brain, and finally produce a sensation." [2] We might have supposed that we were seeing an object, but this is a mere supposition; for what we thought was color is simply the effect of light rays as they stimulate the optical organs and give us a sensation. Since the sensation is regarded as an "effect" of something, we infer an object or agent as its "cause." But if as far as we can ever travel is from one effect to another, we can never know if, in fact, there is a cause. Nor do we have any right, therefore, to do more than assume the existence of a "cause." An assumption, we learn, which is a matter of one's own metaphysics; a choice dictated not by logic but by taste, and where each man is free to name his own brand.

These argument provide grounds, it is alleged, for doubting the existence of material objects, and indeed, the entire "external world." These doubts are fatal thrusts, they pierce the heart of common sense. If we are persuaded by this turn of analysis we must maintain that common sense, if carried out consistently, leads to its own bankruptcy, to self-refutation, and to uncommon non-sense. "Naive realism," to quote the general point being asserted, "leads to physics, and physics, if true, shows that naive realism is false. Therefore naive realism, if true, is false; therefore it is false." [3] And this general formula serves to explain such statements as: "Common sense imagines that when it sees a table it sees a table. This is a gross delusion." [4] or "What Dr. Whitehead calls the 'pushiness' of matter disappears altogether...matter is a convenient formula for describing what happens where it isn't." [5] Yet this analysis which proceeds so admirably to exhibit the inadequacies of common sense is not without its own difficulties. If one holds the existence of (say) the "external world" to be dubious, on the grounds of what "physics says" then he is obliged to doubt the very physical constructions and interpretations which initially provide the instruments by which this scepticism was set loose. One might be suspicious of an analysis which begins by telling us what physics says, and ends by claiming grounds for doubting the existence of the world and, therefore, doubting the very subject-matter of physics and the existence of the things physics talks about. Physics too, like common sense, is then largely a product of illusion. The argument began by an appeal to what physics says; and an argument that must conclude by doubting the assumptions from which it has proceeded is circular. Another difficulty has been put by those who have employed this type of analysis as follows: assuming physics is right, it refutes common sense. How then from false-common sense did true-physics come into being? How is the rise of physics from the bed of naive realism to be explained if analysis leads us to say "Naive realism leads to physics, and physics, if true, shows that naive realism is false. Therefore naive realism, if true, is false; therefore it is false"? To this problem the adherents of this argument have been giving much attention but seem, so far, not to have reached any satisfactory conclusion.

It may be held that this brand of analysis, which has often been called empirical, is, indeed, a strange form of empiricism. For not only are the usual techniques by which empirical verification of assertions is accomplished, made suspect, but a weird animism inhabits this welter of logical construction. This is evident in the notion that explanations and definitions have some charged and intimate relation to the things being explained and defined —to the things being talked about. Hence, change the description of matter, and it suddenly is no longer hard and disappears quite away; or, after reading a passage from Dr. Whitehead the 'pushiness' of one's table suddenly disappears. To learn that on giving the authority on matters physical to the physicist, when we see a table we imagine we see a table and "this is a gross delusion," may delight a poet but is hardly calculated to please a hard headed empiricist.

There is, however, as least one crucial assumption being made in this argument which we have been briefly following—an assumption which never appears explicitly, but serves as a source from which the dramatic and logical force of the argument draws its secret dialectical strength. This assumption is that the *language* of physics, or the more advanced sciences, has in some sense a claim to priority over all other modes of discourse, particularly that of common sense. On this assumption, when common sense language speaks of a table as being a hard, brown, material object, it is deluded. For an analysis of the same object in the language of theoretical physics, the terms "hard," "brown," and "material object" are no longer employed, and are replaced by a precise terminology, facilitated by mathematical techniques and complex theories. The "pushiness" of matter, like "matter" itself does not disappear, but what disappears are these *terms*. The terms disappear when a different language, having a different intent and objective no longer finds such terms convenient in conducting analysis and explanation. Depending on the particular objective, one language may be preferable to another; but to call one therefore true and the other false, is to misconstrue this fact, and to make truth a matter of preference for the language one happens to like.

In the context, then, of ordinary common sense experience, common sense language has its place and serves its purpose. It may well happen that an occasion be such that a more precise, controlled, and refined language is necessary, but this fact does not of itself invalidate the function of common sense language. When a language of one context (specifically developed to deal with the kind of materials and issues of that context) is transferred and imposed on another context the results may be odd and often a travesty. It is a misuse of language and hardly enlightening to inform the lover that all his beloved "really" is, is a "system of electrons and protons in rapid motion, with empty space in between."

These objections are not intended to imply that common sense beliefs and language are not often misleading and vague, indeed they are. Common sense in general, is at least as saturated with the devious and erroneous as it is with the practical and true. I have raised these issues to indicate the kind of interpretation of common sense and science, and the problems generated, which Dewey works against in offering his own formulation and view of the subject.

Dewey's account of common sense takes a course quite different from that which we have been following thus far. In good part common sense receives a formulation different from what is usually has in philosophy, and in turn, is given a more fundamental status. The expression "common sense," Dewey says, "is a usable and useful name for a body of facts that are so basic that without systematic attention to them 'science' cannot exist, while philosophy is idly speculative apart from them because it is then deprived of footing to stand on and of a field of significant application."[6] Quoting the *Oxford Dictionary*, Dewey states what he regards as an expression that admirably fits the case. Here common sense is defined as a name used for "the general sense, feeling, judgment of mankind or of a community...Good sound practical sense...in dealing with everyday affairs."

The *life* of a community consists of its everyday, practical, run-of-the-mill activities. It is in these common life activities that the general over-all ingenuity and practical wisdom of community members is exercised; it is here common sense is located and is found to play, for better or worse, with the materials and forces governing ordinary life. Dewey goes on to say: "As for the word 'sense' joined to 'common,' we note that the dictionary gives as one usage of that word 'intelligence in its bearing on action.' "[7] And in the light of the basic view underlying his discussion of common sense, Dewey might have changed this to read: intelligence in its bearing on transactions. For, it will be remembered, Dewey has described human life, individually and collectively, as consisting of an extensive body of transactions; transactions in which human as well as the non-human are partakers in a give and take togetherness, are *parties* in transactions. An individual, or "thing," can only be understood when it is seen as a participants in a network of transactions. Even in its physical and psychological dimensions life depends on being a party in transactions, to say nothing of the cultural and social and economic conditions partaking in the transactions of living. The individual, along with his fellow beings and non-human things, as they are caught up and participate in transactions are not to be thought of as separate entities, clashing and parting. Individual is not set off from environment with nothing but friction between them: "What is called environment is that in which the conditions called physical are enmeshed in cultural conditions and thereby are more than 'physical' in its technical sense. 'Environment' is not something around and about human activities in an external sense; it is their *medium,* or *milieu,* in the sense in which a *medium* is *inter*mediate in the execution of carrying *out* all human activities, as well as being the channel *through* which they move, and the vehicle *by* which they go on." [8]

On having recognized these general features underlying and essential to common sense, Dewey's further account of the characteristics possessed by common sense may be put as follows. 1) The distinguishing trait of common sense is that it is acquaintance knowledge. "Only by direct active participation in the transactions of living does anyone become *familiarly acquainted* with other human beings and with 'things' which make up the world." [9] Acquaintance knowledge "demarcates the frame of reference of common sense by identifying it with the life actually carried on as it is enjoyed or suffered."

2) Common sense is an affair of concerns: the words "occupied," "engaged," "busied," etc. do more than indicate its flavor, they set forth its subject-matter. For "concern" bespeaks of solicitude and care for that "with which one is occupied and *about* which one is called upon to act." [10] And "concern," Dewey reminds us, in usage means "that one has to do with or has ado with"; *ado* meaning "a doing that is forced on one, a difficulty, trouble." These practical concerns, worked out in action, speech, or thought, are the *things* of these transactions, having human beings as their partners, which make up the entire net-work of human activity. The words "concern," "affair," "care," "thing," Dewey says, "fuse in indissoluble unity which when discriminated are called *emotional, intellectual, practical...*" [11] The first two, emotional and intellectual, being the two marked traits of the practical. It being a matter of a given context, which shall be judged the uppermost or more apparent; a judgment of emphasis, not separation.

In considering the traits that distinguish the subject-matter and procedure of science from that of common sense, Dewey emphasizes that science, too, is a human concern, affair, and occupation. Nor is the difference between science and common sense to be made in terms of "theory" and "practice," if these terms mean intellectual and mental, as against practical and manual operations. Observation of scientific inquiry, as conducted by highly trained persons employing special equipment and technical apparatus, usually carried on in *labor*-atories, hardly warrants the label "intellectual," if this is to imply that little or no practice, or overt activity goes on. To deny the special kind of occupations that go on, the mediation of material devices and technical operation, is to ignore the experimental side of scientific concerns. It is true that pursuits called "intellectual" and "theoretical" certainly go on within any scientific activity; but the status usually ascribed to these particular pursuits gives an interpretation to scientific procedure that is very nearly the equivalent of the claim that wars are fights between generals. A truth, but a short sighted truth which turns so fixedly on one particular feature of an activity that it misses all that is massive and significant. Doing and knowing are both involved in scientific activity; they are both necessary conditions for its existence.

In science as an occupation, a care, knowing is the important consideration. But this fact does not of itself mark science off from common sense, for knowing is as necessary a feature in the concerns of common sense as in science. "But knowing is there for the sake of the *agenda* the *what* and *how* of which have to be studied and to be learned—in short, known in order that the necessary affairs of daily life be carried on. The relation is reversed in science as a concern." [12] "In each case," Dewey says, "doing remains doing and knowing remains knowing." It is the special concern of science and the particular and distinctive concern of common sense "with respect to *what* is done and known, and *why* it is done and known" that renders the subject matters of "the two concerns as different as H_2O is from the water we drink and wash with." [12] Put more roughly, we might say that as a concern, common sense, in its concerns with some given subject-matter, will render and manipulate it according to certain demands—to certain specific concerns of its own. *What* is done and known, and *why* it is done and known, mark the distinctive traits and concerns of common sense, and distinguish it from science and the concerns of science.

If water be the subject matter of some particular concern called "common sense," then the demands of the concern on the subject matter will be the demands of direct and familiar acquaintance. That subject matter will be recognized as the 'stuff' which quenches thirst, "cleans the body, and soiled articles, supports boats," falls from heaven, affects the growth of crops and flowers, is the sportsman's enemy and street-cleaner's friend. Taken as such, this particular subject-matter of common sense has little or nothing to do with the H_2O of scientific concern. Or, more accurately, the particular demands as concerns of common sense (the what and why) have nothing to do with the demands as concerns of science. The demand of each concern renders a particular natural event, in the first case into 'water,' and in the latter case into H_2O. The last named (H_2O), Dewey adds, is *about* the first named, "although what one consists *of* is radically different from what the other consists *of*. The fact that what science is *of* is *about* what common sense subject-matter is *of*, is disguised from ready recognition when science becomes so highly developed that the immediate subject of inquiry consists of what has *previously* been found out. But careful examination discloses that unless the materials involved can be traced back to the material of common-sense concern there is nothing whatever for scientific concern to be concerned with. What is pertinent here is that science is the example, *par excellence*, of the liberative effect of abstraction. Science is *about* in the sense in which 'about' is *away* from and is *of* in which 'of' is off from:—how far off is shown in the case repeatedly used, water as H_2O, where not one single property of use and enjoyment belonging to the former is to be found in the latter. The liberative outcome of the abstraction which is supremely manifested in scientific activity is that transformation of the affairs of common-sense concern which has come about through the vast return c^r ˯ ˙ methods and conclusions of scientific concern in ˙ ˙ ˷ses and enjoyments (and sufferings) of everyday affairs; together with an accompanying transformation of judgment and of the emotional affections, preferences, and aversions of everyday human beings." [13]

I have quoted at length, because it is in this passage (one of the most significant, I think, in Dewey's writings on this subject) that Dewey draws the distinctions he believes exist, between common sense and science. It is well worth observing, in view of our earlier discussion, that Dewey does not set common sense and science against one another. The "water" of common sense is not a delusion, nor is it "really" H_2O. Nor does the description and analysis of a certain natural property, as H_2O, in science, in some sense invalidate or make false the understanding of that property called "water," and all of the enjoyments and sufferings associated with that name and property in common sense life. For, beginning with the materials of common sense and the things of enjoyment and suffering, scientific inquiry, employing specialized technical skills and apparatus, may be led to conclusions and the refinement of the materials controlling attention, having no immediate or direct bearing whatever on common sense concerns.

What scientific inquiries have to tell us about the water of common-sense experience may affect how water is regarded, under certain conditions, as a property of common sense concerns. We learn that water under various circumstances may contain properties of a bio-chemical sort which are harmful to human life. It has only been after certain scientific investigations had worked their effects on common sense knowledge, that the fact that boiling water serves as a medium for sterilizing instruments of all sorts has become a commonly accepted practice and part of everyday knowledge.

The conclusions of scientific inquiries have repercussions on other scientific issues, and in generating new inquiries also return with an increasingly radical force to transform the place and conditions of their origins. The full force of these return waves is felt in their re-working of the inertial mass of common sense. A re-working in which the energies and interests of common sense are rendered articulate and are shorn and liberated from illusion and error.

Dewey has put the matter this way: "1) Scientific subject-matter and procedures grow out of the direct problems and methods of common sense, of practical uses and enjoyments, and 2) react into the latter in a way that enormously refines, expands and liberates the contents and the agencies at the disposal of common sense." [14] The advancement of science reacts on common sense as a transforming and liberating power so that the latter, too, advances.

In spite of this profound and significant interpretation that Dewey gives us of the agencies of common sense and science and their functional interdependence as found exemplified in the living world, certain objections and considerations present themselves. For, it was said earlier that much of what passed for common sense knowledge was uncritical, vague, and often incompatible, or inconsistent. When common sense is thus characterized, or called "naive realism," there seems little place for it in that enterprise which Dewey formulates and describes as common sense. In portraying common sense not only as a going, practical concern, but as the general sense of a community and "good sound practical sense...in dealing with everyday affairs," Dewey is reconstructing common sense and giving it a status which in more traditional language might be called *good* common sense, or *true* naive realism. The implication of this language is that common sense, as we meet it, is to be taken as an inchoate mass of beliefs and prescriptions for action, including a few obsolete but still half-living superstitions, and possessing, along with good sense, a full share of bad, unsound, impractical sense. In characterizing common sense as he does, the claim might be made that Dewey fails to recognize a mass of beliefs which have had, and continue to have, an ill effect on human behavior; bad or unsound beliefs not only have histories, but are also known to have to be influential in the practical concerns and decisions of of daily living. The history of the sciences is full of examples where particular advances in inquiry were met with scorn on the ground that they ran counter to common sense. There are some philosophers today (as well as those few "empirical" scientists in Hitler Germany) who have maintained that Einstein's work in physics cannot be correct because it violates common sense. Now clearly, the "common sense" that constitutes the subject-matter of appeal for the claims in these cases, is not the common sense Dewey is concerned with. Yet this kind of "common sense," if not so called, does not cease to exist, and clamors for recognition. No account of the development of scientific inquiries which have run counter to the funded opinion of the times, can afford to overlook such an influential body of beliefs.

The objection I am raising here poses no serious challenge to Dewey's discussion of common sense and science. But if the objection be sound, it indicates a needed expansion of Dewey's discussion to cover and deal with those common beliefs and attitudes which do possess the characteristics of being "cocksure, vague, and self-contradictory." Dewey's common sense, taken as good, sound, practical sense, is sense which has been singled out and emphasized, with too little comment made on the less admirable "sense" that also thrives in the context of practical concerns and affairs. We may heartily agree that science, rising from the context of common sense, works and transforms those materials through inquiry so that the result is an enlarging and liberating of the agencies of common sense. But this very fact implies that common sense has been enlarged and liberated *from* something. 9nd it is that "something," whatever it be called, that requires candid recognition and inclusion in an account of the on-going concern of science, if that account is to be as significant and forceful as truth to its subject-matter would demand it to be.

What I have been saying so far by no means affects the fundamental thesis that Dewey has in mind, namely "the attainment of unified method means that the fundamental unity of the structure of inquiry in common sense and science be recognized, their difference being one in the problems with which they are directly concerned, not to their respective logics." [15] What seems to be needed is the attainment of a unified logic, a theory of inquiry, which resolves the split (being common to both parties) between common sense procedure and science, or, between the logic of science and the methods of common sense. Dewey has proposed such a unified theory of inquiry, and to it we may now turn.

2.

THE PATTERN OF INQUIRY

I MENTIONED at the beginning of this chapter that there is a series of successive phases or levels to any inquiry. These phases, taken together, constitute the descriptive characteristic, the form or *pattern* of inquiry. Dewey has given us a remarkably explicit formulation of this pattern. Let us proceed to trace this general pattern, before concerning ourselves with some of the particular issues that arise in connection with certain features of that pattern.

Inquiry is defined as *"the controlled or directed transformation of an indeterminate situation into one that is so determinate in its constituent distinctions and relations as to convert the elements of the original situation into a unified whole."*[16] Thinking, insofar as it is a reflective activity, has in all of its flights or units, two boundary limits: it begins with a "perplexed, troubled, or confused situation at the beginning and a cleared-up, unified, resolved situation at the close."[17] It is to be noted that "what is designated by the word 'situation' is *not* a single object or event or set of objects and events. For we never experience nor form judgments about objects and events in isolation but only in connection with a contextual whole...In actual experience there is never any such isolated singular object or event; *an* object or event is always a special part, phase, or aspect, of an environing experienced world—a situation."[18] Consequently, an unsettled or indeterminate situation is one in which "its constituents do not hang together." [19] And inquiry, when it completes it course, results in working the original situation into a unified whole "to the degree in which the operations involved in it actually do terminate in the establishment of an objectively unified existential situation." [19] The successive stages in the progression of inquiry occur as follows.

1) *The indeterminate situation.* Dewey calls this first stage "the antecedent conditions of inquiry." It is pre-reflective in the sense that it precedes inquiry and reflection: for when these begin the situation has started to become determinate in being subjected to inquiry. Inquiry doesn't begin for its own sake, but because the constituents within a situation have become discordant. It is this kind of a situation that evokes inquiry; it is *actually* unsettled, disturbed, uncertain, and potentially *questionable*. It is the whole *situation* which is disturbed, troubled, confused, full of conflicting tendencies, etc. "*We* are doubtful because the situation is inherently doubtful. Personal states of doubt that are not evoked by and are not relevant to some existential situation are pathological." [20] To suppose, therefore, that a situation is doubtful in some "subjective" sense (i.e., that "doubt" is a "state of mind" or an occurrence inside of a human head) is to misread Dewey's entire discussion of the existentially interactive and organic setting of inquiry, and, to overlook his definition of *situation*; a seductive slip which Dewey takes great pains to caution against. It follows that situations which are troubled or disturbed cannot be straightened out by any conceivable manipulation of personal states of mind. To insure against such misinterpretations Dewey writes: "The biological antecedent conditions of an unsettled situation are in-

volved in that state of imbalance in organic-environmental interactions"... and this "state of disturbed equilibration constitutes *need*. The movement towards its restoration is search and exploration. The recovery is fulfillment or satisfaction."[21]

This state of "imbalance in organic-environmental interactions" is, perhaps, the clearest way to describe the antecedent conditions of inquiry. Its biological character is the more apparent when Dewey continues to say: "Every such interaction is a temporal process, not a momentary cross-sectional occurrence. The situation in which it occurs is indeterminate, therefore, with respect to its *issue*." It is *confused* means that "its outcome cannot be anticipated. It is called *obscure* when its course of movement permits of final consequences that cannot be clearly made out. It is called *conflicting* when it tends to evoke discordant responses." [22] The indeterminate or unsettled situation, furthermore, "is not uncertainty at large, it is a unique doubtfulness which makes that situation to be just and only the situation it is." [23] This is a truism, but it follows that "it is this unique quality that not only evokes the particular inquiry engaged in but that exercises control over its special procedures." [24]

In the "interaction of organic responses and environing conditions and their movement toward an existential issue" the conditions for the institution of a problem have been set when the kind of responses the organism is to make is a matter of concern. "Organic interaction becomes inquiry when existential consequences are anticipated," i.e., when environing conditions are examined for what they contribute and when activities of selection and ordering of some, rather than others, of these conditions take place, with a view to actualizing what potentially they reveal and offer in the way of materials for the resolution and settlement of the initial difficulty.

2) *Institution of a problem.* "To see that a situation requires inquiry is the initial step in inquiry." [25] The first result of an indeterminate situation, in giving rise to inquiry, is that the "situation is taken, adjudged, to be problematic." Obviously, if no problem can be instituted, so that the energies and earnest overtness to reach some conclusion find some center and point of vantage from which materials can be gathered—a point which marks the bounds of relevancy as set by a problem—there will be but a blind and futile uncoordinated groping. A problem sets the stage and marks the general area in which inquiry is to work; it is the beginning of the transformation of problematic into determinate situation. And the *way* in which a problem is conceived and set will control suggestions, the relevancy and irrelevancy of hypotheses and the selection of data. On the formulation of the problem will depend the success and adequacy of the entire structure and outcome of the inquiry proceeding from it.

3) *Determination of a problem-solution: hypotheses.* Once the statement of a problematic situation has been formulated in terms of a problem, various possible solutions may be suggested. These are hypotheses: anticipations and forecasts of what, under certain conditions present, will happen if a plan (or suggestion) is acted out. Hypotheses are ideas (or, ideas are hypotheses), they are anticipations of consequences when (or if) a certain action is performed. In this sense Dewey regards ideas or hypotheses, as plans of action. Hypotheses, as they come into play, are not products of pure fancy and imagination. They rise out of the formulation of a problem as well as the conditions which observation secures as the constituents and

traits of the situation. Dewey says: "Statement of a problematic situation in terms of a problem has no meaning save as the problem instituted has, in the very terms of its statement, reference to a possible solution." [26] A situation, which, strictly speaking, is *completely* indeterminate, cannot be worked or transformed even to the extent of being a problem having definite constituents. [26] The preliminary step consists in searching for the constituents of a situation which, as constituents, are located somewhere, and other spatial-temporal and behavioral features may be located as additional features making the situation what it is. "The facts of the case" constitute the observed conditions and they make up the terms of the problem "because they are conditions which must be reckoned with or taken account of in any relevant solution that is proposed." [27] Hypotheses are suggested by this "determination of factual conditions which are secured by observation."

When Dewey says that the statement of a problem "has no meaning save as the problem instituted has, in the very terms of its statement, reference to a possible solution" he is liable to be misunderstood. A statement has reference to a possible solution in the sense that it draws attention to certain facts and materials which any proposed solution, if it is relevant, must take into account. As has already been quoted, these facts "constitute the terms of the problem"; they are the conditions to be reckoned with when possible solutions are being proposed. What Dewey is *not* saying is that the statement of the problem has reference to a solution in the sense that the very formulation of the problem provides a solution—where the word "provides" means that a mere inspection of the statement will somehow yield the secret and conclusion of the problem. A statement has meaning only as it has *reference* to a possible solution, means that the statement indicates the area, the frame of reference, which action, or proposed plans of action, must acknowledge and observe if they are to be relevant possible solutions.

Off-hand and of-the-moment suggestions spring constantly to mind when we are perplexed or troubled. Such suggestions may come on us as sudden flashes, or they may well up and slowly illumine the whole puzzled intermingled pause of responses and conditions seeking some outcome and settlement. They are urges to overt activity, and as they break or dawn upon us they do more than light up the landscape and existing circumstances of our confusion: they are turned on outcomes; they carry hints and promises of solutions; they cut paths through the darkness and switch faintly on objects at the far. end. Yet suggestions may be misleading; their promises cannot be taken on their word alone. Each suggestion has to be "examined with reference to its functional fitness; its capacity as a means of resolving the given situation." [28] When suggestions are so examined they become ideas, hypotheses. "Every idea originates as a suggestion but not every suggestion is an idea." In this examining process some suggestions may be readily dismissed as failing to meet the desired requirements and as the examination proceeds, even some hypotheses or ideas may be eliminated. The examination itself is what Dewey calls reasoning.

4) *Reasoning.* Since ideas are plans of action, proposals for possible solution of a given problem, that plan of action will be their *meaning*. The meaning of an idea is the plan to act in a certain way. The proposal that organic response and function in a problematic situation take a particular direction which will possibly resolve the given situational difficulty, *is* the meaning content of that proposal, plan, or

idea. Here is a fundamental philosophical idea put forth by Dewey, and often associated with what is called "operational meaning." Peirce, no doubt influencing Dewey in this, as in some other respects, had developed a criteria of meaning which (put roughly) holds that the meaning of a statement *is* the sum of its verifiable consequences. Peirce says, for example, that chemistry is concerned with discovering certain kinds of behavior of material substance. And he adds: "And in what does that behavior consist except that if a substance of a certain kind should be exposed to an agency of a certain kind, a certain kind of sensible result *would* ensue, according to our experiences hitherto. As for the pragmaticist, it is precisely his position that nothing else than this can be so much as *meant* by saying that an object possesses a character." [29] We cannot here enter upon an exposition of this fundamental idea as developed by Dewey. And I shall do the position involved the injustice, for the sake of brevity and clarity, of stating it as follows: We study a thing, we recognize it and learn what it means, by its behavior. So we may say: a thing is (or means) what it does. Just as a thing means what its characteristic behavior is in experience and as experienced, so to say an idea is a plan of action for the resolution of a problem-situation, is to say an idea *means* what its plan is—it means what it proposes to do in experience and as experienced.

Reasoning is an examination of these plans; an examination of meanings, "as a result of which we are able to appraise better than we were at the outset, the pertinency and weight of the meaning now entertained with respect to its functional capacity." [30] It is of the nature of plans of action that they are concerned with future states of affairs, affairs not directly present in given existence. Hence, "the meanings which they involve must be embodied in some symbol. Without some kind of symbol no idea; a meaning that is disembodied cannot be entertained or used." [30] Rational discourse is this process which operates with symbols, symbols which, Dewey says, constitute propositions. "The check upon immediate acceptance" of an idea, "is the examination of the meaning as a meaning." But what is an examination of a meaning as a meaning? It consists, Dewey continues, "in noting what the meaning in question implies in relation to other meanings in the system of which it is a member, the formulated relation constituting a proposition. If such and such a relation of meanings is accepted, then we are committed to such and such other relations of meanings because of their membership in the same system." [31] A simple illustration may make this point clear. Suppose a man, on his way to work, discovers that the reason the world looks somewhat hazy to him is not because of climate or the seasonal elements, but because he has forgotten to put on his spectacles. A discordant situation has thus been taken note of, and a statement of the problem-situation might occur as follows: "No wonder things seemed odd, I've forgotten my spectacles." Having located the trouble, the statement also presents certain 'facts of the case.' Suggestions then occur. He might, it occurs to him, return home to look for his spectacles; or he might try to carry on without them; on the other hand, they might be in one of his pockets. Each one of these suggestions may seem worth examining; it might also occur to him that if he didn't read so much, he wouldn't have to be troubled by occurrences like this: but this suggestion is eliminated as irrelevant to the problem.

Our hypothetical man continues to examine these suggestions; he notes what each meaning implies in relation to other meanings in a system of which it is a member. That is, if he should return home, he may find his spectacles but that may involve him in being late to work. On the other hand if he continues on his way he will get to work on time, but be without his spectacles. He notes also that if he acts on the plan of returning home, he is committed to the proposition that his spectacles are, in fact, there to be found. This in turn commits him to related meanings and propositions: If they are to be found at home, then they are not in any of his pockets, nor did he lose them on the way. He is committed to these meanings because they have membership in the same system of meanings. The most convenient plan for him to try out first, is to search his pockets; he may do so, and on not finding what he wants he then considers the other two hypotheses, and the relations each has to other meanings and consequences which are involved when one of these plans is acted on. Having finished this examination, or stage of reasoning, our man has arrived at a plan that he regards as the most relevant and adequate—considering the facts and circumstances involved—for solving his problem. He then proceeds to act it out.

This illustration is offered in an attempt to clarify what Dewey means by a meaning examined for what it implies "in relation to other meanings in the system of which it is a member, the formulated relation constituting a proposition." the end product of such an examination occurs when, "through a series of intermediate meanings, a meaning is finally reached which is more clearly *relevant* to the problem in hand than the originally suggested idea." [32] In the intermediate stages of inquiry, Dewey stresses, facts and meanings function and operate together. Facts give rise to suggestions and meanings, meanings in turn direct the observation and disclosure of other and new facts, which again refine and re-adjust the meanings involved. Thus facts are linked to ideas, ideas lead to observation, and observation leads to new facts and ideas. Facts and meanings are operational in the sense that they are interrelated and interdependent; and in the progression of inquiry the relation of facts and meanings also has a serial progressive course, in which ideas or possible solutions are being formed, refined, and tested.

In scientific inquiry, the relation of meanings to other meanings is often of crucial import in considering the adequacy of some given meaning. That is, in an already established system of meanings or propositions, a given meaning is suspect if it is shown to contradict or be inconsistent with one or more meanings of that system or propositions which are deductive consequences of it. The given meaning is suspect, on the probable grounds, that it is more likely to be in error than a whole set of propositions which follow from and which may in part warrant a law or theory. And should the given meaning prove "stubborn," revisions, rather than a wholesale scrapping of the system, will be the normal procedure. The point here being, that in the case of advanced scientific inquiries the 'relatedness' of a meaning to a system of meaning often takes prior consideration to the practical or experimental consequences of that meaning. This is on the grounds that consistency is not only an ideal but a ruling principle in scientific inquiries, and it is a violation of that principle for both "p" and "not-p" (where p is some proposition) to be accepted as members of the same system. If, therefore p be a meaning or idea in some particular inquiry, and not-p (contradicting p) be either an established part of some theory, or can be shown to be neces-

sary consequence of it, then the validity of p is questionable. The validity of p is questioned, it is true, on what
might be called indirect and probable grounds; it is questioned because it is inconsistent with a theory (or system)
and the evidence warranting p is evidence for a single
proposition, whereas the evidence warranting a theory is
*at leas*t the evidence warranting each one of the propositions which follow deductively from it. And since a theory, if it *is* a theory, will always have more evidence for it
than any single statement, or hypotheses, will have, the
warrantability of any idea may, in part, be judged in
terms of the relation that idea bears to other established
or accepted meanings. This way of judging an idea is, of
course, never more than tentative; but it is a convenient
and initial step in practice. There are exceptions to this
rule of practice and these exceptions sometimes cause mi-
nor upheavals or major revolutions: what had formerly
been regarded as a sound and established system is radically transformed and changed to meet, and account for,
new evidence.

Here, perhaps, we have one characteristic difference between the inquiries of science and those of common sense.
In the examination of a given meaning, or hypotheses,
the consideration of the relation of that meaning to a system of meanings and the relations of meanings to one another is far less extensive and elaborate in common sense
than in scientific procedure. This makes scientific reasoning far more intricate, refined, complex, and abstract
(hence employing highly developed systems of symbols)
than the reasoning, or examination of meanings, bearing
directly on the transactions of everyday practical affairs.
This is not to say that in common sense the examination
of the relations of meanings to other meanings does not

occur. In the illustration of a common sense inquiry and practical concern, it was said that the man, in trying to locate where his spectacles might be found, knew that if they (the spectacles) are to be found at home, then they are not in any one of his pockets, nor did he lose them on the way, etc. A practical proposition, but one which is implicitly supposed valid because it is related to an accepted principle of logic to the effect that a proposition cannot both be true and false. Hence if "the spectacles are to be found in my home" is true, then "the spectacles are not to be found in my home," or "they are here, or there, etc." are false—as any proposition which is a denial of a true proposition is false. Common sense may never make its guiding principles explicit, as a science (or logic) might, but this fact does not mean that such principles are not employed in common sense inquiries. But it is in this concern to find relations among meanings, facilitated by abstract and symbolic manipulations, as well as to make explicit the rules and techniques for these manipulations, that science may be observed to differ in degree (not in kind) from common sense. Because of its very abstractness "where meanings are related to one another on the ground of their character *as* meanings"[33] scientific inquiry is freed from the more direct concerns of the immediate, and freed from the limits of group concerns. It is hence a liberated activity to which the fierce interests and partisan loyalties that assuage the dreaming and desiring human world are markedly irrelevant.

5) *Experiment.* "An hypothesis, once suggested and entertained, is developed in relation to other conceptual structures until it receives a form in which it can instigate and direct an experiment that will disclose precisely those conditions which have the maximum possible force in de-

termining whether the hypothesis should be accepted or rejected." [34] An hypothesis is a plan of action; experiment is the overt activity, the plan acted out. The nature of an experiment, the techniques and apparatus employed and the kind of situation in which the directed action goes on, may vary with different inquiries and the particular problems generating inquiries. The conditions for experiment and the success of the outcome depend, in part, on the initial demands of the whole problematic situation. If the conclusion of an experiment is such that the original problematic situation becomes settled, made coherent, closed, or reaches a solution, the experiment is successful: the plan of action guiding the experiment is shown to be the "answer," the key to the disturbed situation. A successful experiment, then, is one that works an existential change in the whole problematic situation; what had been troubled or unsettled, becomes transformed into a cleared and settled situation. If an experiment fails so to transform the situation which it has been designed, as a means, to settle, then inquiry continues: it may retrace and reexamine its own procedures and develop other hypotheses to be tried out. There is some ambiguity in saying, as one often does, that an experiment settles a situation or is a success. Strictly speaking, the experiment is a success (or not) and settles a situation only in the sense that it discloses whether or not a hypothesis should be accepted or rejected. To say that an experiment is a success is to say that it shows a given hypothesis to be such that the hypothesis solves, or settles, the problem-situation which instigated inquiry. A hypothesis that "works," is a hypothesis that experiment, or the overt activity of carrying it out, makes evident, "satisfies," the demands set by the troubled situation in leaving the situation complete and no longer troubled. But the terms "works" and "satisfies," Dewey has patiently made quite clear, do not in any sense refer to private states of mind or to personal whim and fancy.

When a plan of action *works,* when it satisfies the conditions of a problem-situation and one concludes that a plan of action is warranted, does this mean warrantability is a mere matter of "what works for me," or that whatever satisfies *me* is therefore warranted? Clearly not, and nowhere in Dewey's writings will such a position, which many critics have ascribed to him, be found to be maintained.[35] The difficulty here, of course, arises when one kind of meaning of "satisfaction" is taken as the only meaning. "Satisfaction" is held to mean a personal and private state of comfort. It then follows that Dewey's notion of a "true" plan of action as one satisfying certain objective troubled conditions, is truth reduced to personal states of mind; truth being whatever I find comforting, whatever I choose it to be. If this be the only fixed meaning of "satisfy," then Dewey should be obliged to change an occasional usage of that word in discussing his theory of truth or the outcome of inquiry. But one might as well say, for example, when the military informs a man that he has *satisfied* the conditions for induction into the army, that he has pleased the officers in charge to the extent that they find him personally comforting and therefore accept him for military service. This is hardly an accurate description of the facts. For what does happen in such cases is that, unfortunately, the man in question has met certain objective conditions and standards of bodily health and minimum intelligence which are prerequisites for the conduct of warfare. It would be quite contrary to fact to speak of *satisfying* these standards and conditions as a satisfaction in some personal and private sense. Just as it would be contrary to the actual procedures in the sciences when a theory or hypothesis is said to be satisfactory (or to satisfy the facts) , to regard this as meaning that the theory or hypothesis is comforting or pleasing to some individual person.

The prerequisites then, which determine whether or not a hypothesis is satisfactory, are in no way to be construed as "subjective," "mental," or private. If one remembers how Dewey has defined a situation in general, and especially a problematic situation, the above point is evident if not redundant.

6) *Inquiry concluded and warranted assertion.* When inquiry comes to a close a problematic situation becomes settled. "Judgment may be identified as the settled outcome of inquiry. It is concerned with the concluding objects that emerge from inquiry in their status of being conclusive." [36] "Judgment is transformation of an antecedent existentially indeterminate or unsettled situation into a determinate one." [37] "It is this resulting state of actual affairs—this changed situation that is the matter of the final settlement or judgment." [38] Though Dewey never traces to any great extent the relation of judgments to warranted assertions (or vice versa) I may, without too much danger of error, put the matter briefly as follows. On the basis of these above statements, one might say that warranted assertions are the articulated, or discursive representatives of judgments. Judgment, or final judgment, would thus be regarded as the overt act—the decision taken and carried out—when the energies and resources of inquiry have been ordered and brought to the point where action is ripe and ready. This final action being judgment, it, along with the inquiry producing it, warrants an assertion. "Judgment," Dewey says, "as finally

made, has *direct* existential import." [39] And if judgment *is* the "transformation of an antecedent" unsettled situation into a determinate one, then judgment is the movement, or act as performed. For how else, but by movement and deliberate action can a situation be *transformed*?

There are, no doubt, certain difficulties involved in what I have been saying, and supposing, thus far about judgment, but we must pass them by if we are to proceed to the issues facing us. It might be mentioned, in passing, however, that Dewey does not always discuss judgment in such a way that it is easily identifiable with these statements concerning judgment as the final active settling of a troubled situation. Dewey's basic illustration of judgment is drawn from the procedure of a case of law. A man is sentenced, and the sentence, as carried out, is a case of judgment. But this is unfortunate, because his illustration leaves one wondering where a warranted assertion is relevant, or even what kind of warranted assertion could be formulated. And the fact that law is often called a deductive procedure (rightly or wrongly) at least indicates much to be cleared up by way of the analogy before legal investigations and courtroom procedure clearly illustrates a theory of judgment common to all inquiries—particularly those of science and common sense. But let us return to the issues at hand.

A warranted assertion is a statement, or formulation, of that plan and action which have brought inquiry to a close. The statement, belief, assertion, etc., is *warranted* only as it is the outcome, the product of inquiry. Inquiry is the condition which warrants assertions, beliefs, etc. What is ordinarily called a "true statement," Dewey calls a *warranted assertion*. And what is usually called a theory of truth, for Dewey constitutes a description and account of those existential conditions and the operations performed that generate warranted assertions. When pressed, Dewey has called his 'theory of truth' a correspondence theory. But *correspondence* not in the sense of classical Realism or any of the newer brands, but "correspondence in the operational sense it bears in all cases except the unique epistomological case of an alleged relation between a 'subject' and an 'object'; the meaning, namely, of *answering*, as a key answers to conditions imposed by a lock, or as two correspondents 'answer' each other; or, in general, as a reply is an adequate answer to a question or a criticism—as, in short, a *solution* answers the requirements set of a problem." [40]

In this theory, Dewey holds, both partners in 'correspondence' are not only necessary, but both are in experience and are in the transaction which comes to a conclusion, a settlement. It is, quite strictly, a *co*-respondence theory. For it is a theory which regards a hypothesis as warranted (or true) when it, as a plan, matches or meets the existent conditions set by a problem; that which is asserted as warranted is that which, by means of inquiry, constitutes a *response* to those conditions of a problematic situation in a way that settles, unifies, and resolves them, and is, thereby, a solution to the original difficulty.

There is one direct consequence of this theory which allies it with certain accepted procedures in the sciences. That is when a hypothesis (or idea) or "plan is acted upon *it guides us truly or falsely.*" "The adverb 'truly' is more fundamental than either the adjective, true, or the noun, truth. An adverb expresses a way, a mode of acting." [41] Since ideas are claims that action of a certain stated kind is the means to clearing up a specific problem-situation, it is often the case that some ideas only partially live up to their claims; they may settle a troubled situation but only in part. These ideas are clearly less 'good,' 'workable,' or 'true' than an idea which does clear up a specific situation in *all* of its constituent parts. So it may be that a given problem generates an inquiry which in turn produces a plan of action which fails to settle completely that problem. Other more extensive inquiries are the obvious demand, but until a more satisfactory plan or outcome is arrived at, in lieu of nothing better, if the problem still needs attention, the plan which is partially satisfactory may be retained as a rough working hypothesis. As inquiries progress, they may come ever closer to producing that desired judgment (or final plan of action) which will settle the entire troubled situation. But this is an ideal which practice works towards, and which in some cases may never be entirely realized. And it is also the case that no conclusion of inquiry is intrinsically exempt from a conditional or provisional status; their fate is always subject to the determinations and possible revisions which further inquiries may warrant.

These two fundamental characteristics: the progressive and continuous nature of inquiries and the provisional status of their results, achieve a significant place in Dewey's writings. They also are to be found in Peirce's definition of *truth*, which Dewey quotes with approval, particularly the following: "Truth is that concordance of an abstract statement with the ideal limit towards which endless investigation would tend to bring scientific belief, which concordance the abstract statement may possess by virtue of the confession of its inaccuracy and one-sidedness, and this confession is an essential ingredient of truth." [42]

In conclusion, we may ask, what does it mean to say that

such and such an idea is one "warranting an assertion"? We saw that with the occurrence of problematic situations, inquiry takes place, and in turn generates ideas, or plans for settling those situations. The validity of those ideas will depend on, and be determined by, their consequences (either as anticipated or actually realized) as these consequences do, or do not, settle the problem. An idea, once acted out, which does satisfy the problematic conditions for which it was designed, may be said to be warrantably assertable. Inquiry, we said, *warrants* assertions. The idea itself is a plan or prescription to act or respond to the given situation in a specific way: it is, when formulated in symbols, (i.e., as a proposition) a statement of a set of operations. A warranted assertion is an assertion to the effect that such and such a set of operations, such and such an idea, *is,* or will be, the solution or settlement of such and such a problem. It is not entirely clear, from his discussions of the notion of warranted assertions, to what extent Dewey means these assertions to be statements or formulations in symbols. He occasionally speaks of these "assertions" as if they were, in some sense of assertion, more than linguistic or symbolic devices. He may mean an assertion to be more than the formulation or statement that a state of affairs possesses certain characteristics. It might be that the additional sense of "assertion" that Dewey intends is that sense in which businessmen advise young men that if they are to get ahead in the world, they must *assert* themselves. But, on the whole, Dewey's meaning of "assertion" seems, as against this latter usage of the word, to be intended to indicate the formulation or symbolization of plans of action warranted by inquiry.

We may note that Dewey's notion of warranted assertability, if it can be rightly called a theory of truth, is a theory which is one kind of verifiable theory of truth. For it is that idea, which reflection and experiment terminating in judgment have verified as a solution to a problem, that is warrantably assertable.

3.

CONCLUDING REMARKS

I HAVE been concerned in these pages to trace the pattern of inquiry as it takes place in the matrix of common sense activities and in the related but more refined disciplines known as science. In spite of the modern propensity to talk about science and scientific method, few accounts have done justice to that method as actually exemplified in those procedural activities (in the way problems are investigated and conclusions reached) in the various sciences. If the accounts of scientific conduct and controlled reflective thinking have been slight, still less has been said of the implication of this method and what it promises when once employed in the wider domains of cultural and social affairs and concerns. To these statements, Dewey is an outstanding exception: nowhere in modern thought has the scientific or experimental method been subjected to such a thorough-going formulation and description, a description not only drawing together the biological, psychological and social considerations involved, but also presenting the implications of this method to those various domains as well as to philosophy and human conduct in the world at large. Before turning to certain problems in the above account of Dewey's logical theory one ought, I think, do it the justice of recognizing it as the most extensive, persuasive, and articulate formulation of what reflective thinking is, of the scientific method, and the widespread consequences of that method for human affairs that has yet been accomplished. This much should be kept in mind, I think, in view of the fact that in what follows it is my intention to examine critically some very serious difficulties to be found in Dewey's theory of inquiry. As Professor Hook says, "Dewey's logical theory is the most ambitious attempt ever made to formulate the rationale of modern scientific method." [43]

CHAPTER III.

THE THEORY OF INQUIRY EXAMINED

INTRODUCTORY EXPLANATION

As THE TITLE indicates, I propose now to examine three aspects of the pattern of inquiry. In a very general sense attention will be focused upon the nature of inquiry as it is betrayed to human recognition by three fundamental characteristics:—characteristics located in the initial, intermediate and final phases respectively of the process of inquiry. To have been able to describe what activity occurs when men move from the irritation circumstances making up a problem to the arrival at a solution, a closing of the problem, is an intellectual feat of the first magnitude. To have formulated the description of that activity, its genesis and terminal effects as seen taking place in and among and along with those conditions and traits making up the natural world, as a *theory* —an articulate account of the process and all of the subsidiary details involved—is as striking an accomplishment as can be found in the history of philosophy. This is not intended either as idle or extravagant praise for what Dewey has done. The theory of inquiry as he has formulated it, if it is not a revolution in thought, is certainly such a fundamental re-evaluation and comprehensive re-construction in thought that contemporary eyes lacking historical perspective, can hardly be but half blind to the full significance of what has happened in front of them. There are few in this age, however, who can fail to see how the scientific method of thinking has been transforming men, institutions and the world at large. When this same method is no longer regarded as the peculiar possession of the natural sciences and becomes extended into all domains of living where free intelligence is the ruling principle and method of conduct, then perhaps the merits of Dewey's labors can be adequately judged.

In being necessarily limited to a near-sighted view of what Dewey has done we need not wholly suspend judgment nor need we be silent about some obtruding part or element in the theory that strikes us as discordant simply because the theory as a whole seems so well constructed and on such solid ground. Taking inquiry as a natural process and considering the pattern of that process as Dewey has formulated it, an examination, for all the ocular restrictions put upon it may nonetheless reveal genuine problems to be reckoned with. The following discussion is the product of one such examination. Three problems are dealt with and each problem is located at the very heart of Dewey's account of the three fundamental and characteristic features of inquiry mentioned above. More specifically, Dewey has written (three years after the *Logic* had appeared) that his position is "that all knowledge or warranted assertion depends upon inquiry and that inquiry is, truistically connected with what is questionable. . ." * "Inquiry begins in an indeterminate situation." ** He goes on to say "(i) that knowledge (in its honorific sense) is in every case connected with inquiry; (ii)

that the conclusion or end of inquiry has to be demarcated from the intermediate means by which inquiry goes
forward to a warranted or justified conclusion; that (iii)
the intermediate means are formulated in discourse, i.e.,
as propositions, and that as such they have the properties
appropriate to means (viz., relevancy and efficacy—including economy)." *** This statement of Dewey's admirably
sets the stage for the following discussion. The three
points emphasized in what he has said here constitute the
subject matter of this chapter.

I will be concerned with Dewey's theory of 1) the indeterminate situation; 2) proposition, and 3) the concluding stage of inquiry. In each of these three fundamental
parts of his theory, Dewey has put forth a very original and
significant line of thought. Rather than dealing peacemeal
with various problems and issues and with one or another of the many suggestive themes running through the
Logic, I propose to consider in a somewhat concentrated
fashion these three topics.

Having made this much of a selection of our subject matter, the issues to be dealt with become readily apparent. In
considering what Dewey has to say concerning the indeterminate situation, the crucial problem arises as to whether the way in which Dewey has formulated the essential
characteristics of these situations does full justice to the
empirical temper of his own approach. I shall try to
show first, that Dewey's description and account of these
situations is empirically inadequate. Secondly, I will suggest a revised formulation which gives the description of
these situations an empirically determinate meaning. I
will attempt to formulate what an indeterminate situation
is in such a way that the characteristics asserted to be possessed by such situations can be determined (by empirical

operations of observation of some kind) to exist or not. The second part of the discussion concerns "the intermediate means by which inquiry goes forward to a warranted or justified conclusion." This requires consideration specifically of what Dewey has to say as to the nature of propositions. The outstanding problem facing us here is Dewey's insistence that propositions do not possess the properties of truth or falsehood. I will consider this thesis and attempt to show that the reasons Dewey offers for maintaining this position are insufficient. Assuming for the moment that what I shall try to prove in this section is correct, the discussion would then seem to be largely of a negative sort. It may be well to state why I propose to pursue this matter in this way and why the rsults we shall find are only *prima facie* negative.

As we have occasion to say later on, the view that propositions are neither true nor false, if it could be shown to be true or even probable, has very unpleasant consequences for a great deal of what is generally regarded as established parts of empirical and logical analysis. Many of the achievements in the analysis of empirical procedure as well as the formalization of language are swept away if this doctrine were shown to be true. Unpleasant consequences do not constitute a refutation of a doctrine; but they give us at least pragmatic reasons for hoping the doctrine is false as well as for trying to show it to be false. In the case of Dewey, however, this problem is of a special kind. For Dewey's concern to regard propositions as neither true nor false does not seem to stem from the theory of inquiry as he develops it, nor does this view seem to be logically dictated by any of the other features within the theory as they are formulated and explained. Dewey's concern seems to be to avoid certain epistemological and philosophical constructions that have been erected on the initial ground that propositions are either true or false. He may be quite justified in wishing to avoid such elaborations. In proposing to show that Dewey's rejection of the notion that propositions are true or false is not warranted, I do not intend to be taken as advocating some special epistemological theory. This discussion then is negative only in a relative sense. When it is considered that the view that propositions are true or false does not endanger or have any serious consequences for the other parts of Dewey's theory, the discussion has the value of shearing away an unnecessary and precarious commitment. If I am correct, the result of this analysis may be regarded as providing grounds for thinking that the weighty reasons for accepting the doctrine that propositions are true or false do not, in the discussion of these intermediate means of inquiry, however, I will deal first with the various kinds of propositions and their functions. We shall have to face some issues arising in connection with what these various kinds of propositions *are* in Dewey's theory. These issues will have to be considered before we may turn to the problem of the truth and falsehood of propositions.

The third part of the following discussion concerns the conclusions of inquiry. Here the crucial question immediately appears as to what Dewey means by his constant emphasis that the conclusions of inquiries effect an existential transformation and problem with which inquiry deals. The discussion of this problem will in turn suggest a reformation of Dewey's position.

It is with these three fundamental phases of the pattern of inquiry then, that the following will be devoted; and specifically to the problems, and in the order, stated above. Certain other related issues may have to be introduced, but they will receive our attention only insofar as they contribute to the specific problems to be dealt with.

The following discussion will proceed in this order: Section 1. The Problematic Situation. Section 2. Hypotheses and Propositions; where the topics to be discussed in the order of their headings will be as follows: A. particular propositions; B. universal propositions; C. a suggestion concerning generic and universal propositions; and D. an appraisal of Dewey's general theory of propositions. From thence we shall proceed, finally, to a discussion of Section 3. The Existential Transformations Wrought By the Conclusions of Inquiries.

SECTION 1.
THE PROBLEMATIC SITUATION.

THE frequent observation that Dewey's logical theory is primarily a biological account of how human beings adjust themselves to a changing and precarious world is not wholly unwarranted. For it is to be noticed, in spite of significant passages concerning the social features of inquiries, that Dewey tends to emphasize the indeterminate situation as one of imbalance in the interactions of organism and environing conditions—the blockage of ordinary behavior and the need on the part of the organism, by means of responses, to settle and adjust to the problematic. As I have already quoted to some extent I will only repeat one passage. "The immediate *locus* of the problem concerns, then, what kind of responses the organism shall make. It concerns the interaction of organic responses and environing conditions in their movement toward an existential issue." [1] Now not only is an indeterminate situation one of a falling out of an organism with the run of things, but when it is characterized because, being indeterminate, as doubtful, doubt is not to be attributed as a peculiar quality or state of the organism alone. To say the situation is doubtful, disturbed, troubled, confused, is to say that a "contextual whole" has these attributes or characteristics, and an organism has them only insofar as it is a constituent within that situation. "The habit of the disposing of the doubtful as if it belonged only to *us* rather than to the existential situation in which we are caught and implicated is an inheritance from subjectivistic psychology."[2] Now it is granted that there are serious difficulties and problems which are created and multiply when an explanation employing the principles and techniques of a 'subjectivistic psychology' of doubting, thinking, and inquiry is attempted. The history of philosophy as well as psychology exhibits ample evidence of the host of complexities in which investigations of this sort have become submerged, and the elaborate and often fanciful flights which have been taken in the struggle to escape the perplexing and threatening issues that are consequences not so much of the problem being investigated, as of the kind of assumptions which are made and the way the problem is conceived—consequences born from the very nature of the investigation itself, not from the issues to which it is addressed. It is safe to say that any inquiry is doomed from the beginning, if, as it progresses it becomes increasingly necessary to deal with problems which result from the very assumptions which have been made in the starting of the inquiry. Or put perhaps more succinctly: an inquiry which confuses and cannot disentangle the problem for which it was initially generated from problems arising from its own methods and assumptions, is an inquiry which has lost its direction. I would not want to be understood as saying, however, that an inquiry which, however laboriously, comes to strange or odd conclusions is to be thereby dismissed as false. The point here, and I suspect the point Dewey is concerned with, is that explanations resulting from subjectivistic psychological investigations are construed and formulated in a surprisingly unempirical manner. They are suspicious, not directly because of the apparent paradoxical epistomological problems that they raise, but because of the largely dialectical manner in which they have been conducted, empirical verification is difficult if not impossible.

In granting this much, however, we are not relieved of certain difficulties in Dewey's own analysis. So scrupulously does he wish to avoid the identification of doubting and the indeterminate with personal states of mind, or as affairs within an organism, that he perhaps tends to overemphasize the situational or contextual nature or meaning of these terms. After all it is organisms which do the inquiring; and it very well to say that a *situation* is doubtful, but of all the constituent parts of that situation only those which are human organisms (assuming for the sake of argument that only human organisms can make inquiries) will be observed to move with any sign of intent to unify or settle or conclude that doubtful situation. It would be the height of folly to accuse Dewey of denying these statements, yet it is significant to note that his major definition of inquiry makes no direct mention of an organism as the agent who instigates the transformation of an indeterminate situation into a determinate and unified one. I am not proposing this as grounds for a serious objection. For example, one might be tempted to think up an illustration of a situation which was troubled or discordant and where by chance an element was introduced which resolved or unified that situation, but where throughout no human organism was present. One might ask triumphantly if this was a case of inquiry since the example seems to meet the requirements set by Dewey's definition. This triumph is destined to be short-lived, however, for there is in Dewey's definition of *'situation'* at least an implicit requirement that one of the constituents making up a situation be a human organism. This would seem apparent when he writes, for example: *"An* object or event is always a special part, a phase, or aspect, of an environing *experienced* world—a situation." [3] The word 'experience' means that a situation to be a situation must include an experiencing organism, and this in turn saves Dewey's definition of inquiry from the charge that inquiries might conceivably occur without the presence of human organisms doing the inquiring. The point to which I wish to draw attention runs somewhat deeper than this, and is difficult to state in a manner which does justice to Dewey's discussion of the nature of indeterminate situations.

We may approach the matter as follows. Dewey writes "the original indeterminate situation is not only 'open' to inquiry, but is open in the sense that its constituents do not hang together." [4] Or again in speaking of indeterminate situations as "troubled, disturbed, ambiguous, confused, full of conflicting tendencies, obscure, etc.," Dewey adds, "it is the *situation* that has these traits. *We* are doubtful because the situation is inherently doubtful." [5] But we may ask: in what sense is it significant to assert that the constituents of a situation hang together or do not hang together? Does the phrase "hang together" as it is employed here have a determinate or fixed meaning so that in the explanations or description of situations in general, where the constituents are asserted to hang together, as distinguished from other situations where they do not hang together, the operational interpretation of "hang together" is such that something significant has been asserted? The same question may be asked of the terms "troubled, disturbed, ambiguous, confused, full of conflicting tendencies, obscure, etc." Ordinarily we know what it means to say that something is troubled, disturbed, ambiguous, confused, etc. And for the most part these terms are intended to refer to the state of a living creature. We say he is disturbed, his argument ambiguous, and we are confused etc. But this ordinary tendency to confine the usage of such terms to display or characterize behavioral features of an organism seems clearly at odds with the usage Dewey has in mind. For the start of an inquiry might be then described in this way: the constituents of a situation have become so arranged that an organism finds itself troubled, confused, etc. If asked to define what we meant by 'troubled' or 'confused' we might give specifications of characteristic overt behavior and certain physico-chemical activities in an organism, all of which satisfy the employment of these terms. But the meanings of these terms are fixed by having references to certain functions of living organisms. When, however, Dewey says *"we* are doubtful because the situation is inherently doubtful" whatever this might mean, it certainly doesn't mean what is ordinarily meant by "doubtful." And the fact that one indeterminate situation can be characterized by a variety of names is of little value if no fixed operational meaning is given to these names.

It may be argued, however, that in some sense we do know what Dewey means when he talks about inherently doubtful and indeterminate situations. Dewey has said that his own use of the terms unsettled, troubled, perplexed, etc. was "in the hope that some adjective might induce readers to call up for themselves the kind of situation to which the word 'indeterminate' is applied in connection with inquiry."[6] And in this same context he has said "for no word can describe or convey a *quality*. This statement is, of course, as true of the quality *indeterminate* as it is of the qualities *red, hard, tragic,* or *amusing."* [7] This, as it stands, is an unhappy state of affairs to have to begin from in describing "the necessary condition of cognitive operations of inquiry." [8] But to use a distinction Dewey himself has employed, we can say that the quality indeterminate as *had,* or as directly experienced, or sensed, cannot be conveyed by words. No discourse can reproduce what is enjoyed or suffered as our senses play on the immediate world. No discourse about toothaches can reproduce what toothaches are as sensed or directly experienced. Yet in distinction from things as had, words do convey information about things as *known*. Qualities as known, will be what analysis and empirical investigation have to tell us about them and this includes qualities like red, hard, tragic, amusing, and, presumably, indeterminate. If therefore the notion of indeterminate situations is to have the status of a significant empirical account of the antecedent condition of inquiry, it must lend itself to formulation and interpretation having empirical significance. One may feel he knows what it means to call an indeterminate situation troubled or confused etc., by knowing what these terms mean when applied to human organisms. By a kind of poetic extension he may then attribute these human qualities to the environment and the world at large. But this is hardly warranted by empirical procedure; it is animism at

The criticism here, if it is at all just, rests on a now familiar but significant methodological principal. It might be put roughly as follows: descriptions or explanations of states of affairs are incomplete if the reference system (or criteria) from which these descriptions are made are not themselves specified. On this principle to assert that a situation is inherently doubtful, like asserting a body to be of an inherently rapid velocity, is meaningless. Suppose we eliminate the word "inherent" and say a situation is doubtful, perplexed, confused, etc. Now the problem is, from what criteria, point of view, or relative to what system of reference, is the situation to be understood as possessing these characteristics? Clearly the question as it stands cannot be answered unless some fixed meaning is assigned to these terms (doubtful, troubled, etc.) so that the characteristics asserted of a situation may be determined to exist or not.

We may notice that the various terms Dewey employs in characterizing an indeterminate situation seem to fall into two general classes. Terms like "troubled, disturbed, ambiguous, confused, full of conflicting tendencies, obscure, etc." seem for the most part, as we have suggested, to derive their meaning by having reference to the behavior of living organisms. We might call them *behavioral* terms; they find their meaning in biological and psychological contexts. On the other hand, terms like "inbalance," "unsettled," "open," "not hanging together," seem to have meaning in contexts where some kind of physical operations of measurement and determination are implied. We might call these latter *physical* terms. We might then say that an indeterminate situation is such that from a bio-psychological reference system certain constituents within that situation will be found to exhibit properties which may be defined in physical terms. Is this an elaborate but trivial suggestion? I think not. For if what has been proposed as a rough procedural hypothesis is at all warranted certain consequences follow as to how we are to describe or discourse about indeterminate situations.

It follows, for example, that it is a mistake to describe these situations as over-all or existentially and entirely doubtful, troubled, confused, open, unsettled, etc. For these terms, as they stand, have no fixed meaning. It is also the case that to say "we are doubtful because the situation is inherently doubtful" would have to be revised to say "we possess characteristics defined by behavioral terms, because the situation possesses characteristics defined by physical terms;" or, more generally, "we are doubtful because the situation is unsettled, open, not hanging together (whatever *physical* term is chosen)." But to say we are doubtful, troubled, confused, because the situation is doubtful, troubled, confused (where the *same* terms are used and no distinction between behavioral and physical characteristics is made) is a confusion in language and meaning. It also follows, from what has been said, that it is perfectly legitimate to say *we* are doubtful, in the sense that it is human organisms that do the doubting, where doubting is defined as a certain kind of organic behavior, and that entire situations as such are not doubtful, perplexed, troubled, etc. And I should say that the acceptance of the view that it is constituent human beings who doubt, are troubled and confused, etc., and not entire situations, does not, therefore, necessarily entail the acceptance of a subjectivistic psychology. For it would have to be demonstrated first that the acceptance of the latter position is the only possible alternative to the non-acceptance of Dewey's position.

We may notice, finally, that the revision I have been suggesting brings Dewey's position more into accord with common linguistic usage than his own formulation (though this single point would in itself hardly warrant the revision I am suggesting is needed). Suppose, for example (and I draw from actual experiments conducted in Chicago), we place a child in a maze. The child and the various conditions imposed by the maze make up the situation. The child may wander a bit, his behavior may be observed to be perplexed and confused. At some point he grasps the trouble. He locates the problem and inquiry (in this case the active planning of how to get out of the maze) may be said to begin. But let us consider this stage antecedent to inquiry. This is an indeterminate situation. But if it be described as troubled, confused, perplexed, to what constituents of the situation do these terms meaningfully apply? Can we say the conditions imposed by the maze have these characteristics? Only in one clear sense: we observe that the child exhibits these characteristics and with respect to *his* relation to the maze, *he* is troubled, confused, perplexed, etc.

I will offer one other example by way of indicating certain difficulties involved in Dewey's formulation of indeterminate situations. Suppose we consider a case where in ordinary speech, unsophisticated by philosophic interests, one might say: "I see a red object." Now an analysis of that particular occurrence may reveal it to be a complex and intricate affair, involving a physical object possessing certain properties, and a human organism possessing appropriate sensory organs, etc., certain relations existing between organism and object, the specification of a number of other necessary conditions of the occurrence, such as the presence of light, and so on. All of these conditions may be regarded as making up the constituents of this situation innocently asserted as "I see a red object."

One may readily grant that seeing a red object involves a number of physical and organic conditions, and all of these various conditions may make up the *situation*. But on granting this, would anything be gained by holding that since seeing red involves physical and organic conditions making up a certain situation, one should say "*we* see red because the situation is red"? Would not this be an abuse of language to the extent that there is some question as to whether anything meaningful has been said at all? Because "I see a red object" involves a situation, does it follow that this means I see or perceive red (or a color) because the situation is red (or colored)? I suggest the following as a way in which the same facts can be re-stated. "I see a red object" would be regarded to mean: I am part of a situation possessing certain physical conditions making up what is referred to as "red object," and certain organic or behavioral conditions are also present and referred to as "I see" or "I am seeing." Thus I see red because certain physical and behavioral conditions of a certain sort make up this situation. But it would be meaningless, as it stands, to say I see red, because the situation is inherently red.

In the light of the foregoing, then, I would be inclined to urge the changes suggested above in describing and formulating what is to be meant by indeterminate situations. For if I am correct, such a revision in terminology and procedure yields a more clear and empirically significant manner in which these situation are to be described, located, and understood.[9]

SECTION 2.

HYPOTHESES AND PROPOSITIONS.

I WANT to turn to certain issues involved in the third stage in the pattern of inquiry: that of the formation of hypotheses as initial plans of action for the resolution of a problem. What has been said in chapter two as to the pattern of inquiry may be regarded as a very general account of the function and role of hypotheses in inquiry. It will be remembered that it was stated there, in a rather incidental fashion, that when the meaning content of ideas or hypotheses is being developed as an intermediate stage in inquiry, symbolization is required. The meaning content of hypotheses, when symbolized, Dewey says, takes the form of what he calls *propositions*. With the possible exception of his idea of warranted assertibility, nowhere in his discussion of logic does Dewey depart more from commonly acepted notions and understandings than in his formulation of the place and meaning of propositions in logical theory. The usual definition of a proposition as a statement which possesses the characteristic of being either true or false (and its truth or falsehood being determined either empirically or formally) is rejected by Dewey. In its place he offers a definition of what he means by 'proposition' which is a consequence of the function and traits exhibited by those features of inquiry that are instrumental or means to conclusions. It is to these intermediate features, operating to bring inquiry to some conclusion, that Dewey claims the term 'proposition' rightfully belongs. In view both of this radical departure from what is usually understood and meant by a proposition in logical theory, as well as certain of the original features contained in Dewey's theory of propositions, some discussion of what Dewey's theory means and includes is necessary before we can turn to its attendant problems and merits.

Inquiry concludes, we have noticed, in the settlement of an indeterminate or problematic situation. The closing stoge of inquiry, its settled outcome, Dewey calls a *judgment*. "Final judgment is attained through a series of partial judgments." [10] Factual and perceptual material and ideational or conceptual rules and principles are arranged and ordered by this series of partial judgments until inquiry has become so ordered that the process of actual set- and ordered by this series of partial judgments until in- is a settlement. The case is disposed of; the disposition takes effect in existential consequences." [11] Final judgment offers the grounds or basis for warranted assertions. Hence propositions, Dewey writes, "are logically distinct from judgments, and yet are the necessary logical instrumental- ities of reaching final warranted determination or judg- ment. Only by means of symbolization (the peculiar dif- ferentia of propositions) can direct action be deferred until inquiry into conditions and procedures has been instituted... Propositions as such are, consequently, pro- visional, intermediate and instrumental. Since their sub- ject-matter concerns two kinds of means, material and procedural, they are of two main categories: (1) Existen- tial, referring directly to actual conditions as determined by experimental observation, and (2) ideational or con- ceptual, consisting of interrelated means, which are non- existential in content in *direct* reference but which are applicable to existence through the operations they repre- sent as possibilities." [12] Since these two types of proposi- tions constitute the material and procedural means, "they form the fundamental divisions of labor in inquiry." [13]

A. PARTICULAR PROPOSITIONS

The above categories are the basic distinctions in kinds of propositions. But Dewey includes as sub-classes the following: of existential propositions there are 1) particular; 2) singular; 3) generic; 4) contingent conditional; 5) matter-of-fact or contingent disjunctive. Of the class of ideational or universal propositions there are: 1) hypothetical; 2) disjunctive. There is another class which Dewey calls relational propositions, a class which has properties possessed by both of the above classes. Now these categories and sub-classes denote or designate, presumably, certain distinct traits or features of those operations which enable inquiries to reach conclusions. Just how distinct and how exhaustive of inquiries these above-stated features may be is by no means easily determined. When we turn, for example, to Dewey's discussion of the first of these propositions grouped under the general heading of existential propositions, namely particular propositions, certain difficulties immediately beset us. Dewey says of these "they are propositions which qualify a singular, *this*, by a quality proceeding from an operation performed by means of a sense organ—for example, 'this is sour, or soft, or red, etc.' The word '*is*' in such instances as these has existential force not that of timeless (because strictly logical) copula." And he adds significantly "'this is sour' means either that the actual performance of an operation of tasting has produced that quality in immediately experienced existence, or that it is predicted that if a certain operation is performed it will produce a sour quality." [14]

Now these propositions are important for they serve, Dewey tells us, to represent the first stage in the determination of a problem. They supply the data which indicate the kind of problem the situation presents, as well as the sort of evidence available for formulating a testing of the proposed solution. Yet one must observe from the start that a proposition of the sort "this is red," does not as it is formulated, strictly speaking, yield itself to any specific determinate property. For as it is thus formulated it is difficult indeed to see how such a proposition indicates the sort of problem, or the sort of evidence a particular inquiry will be concerned with, until the term '*this*' of the proposition has some specified meaning. Before the proposition can be regarded to indicate anything definite and hence be of significance in an inquiry the conditions which are designated by the term 'this' have to be specified in a manner that makes it understood what conditions are included and what are excluded when it is said that "this is red." In the terminology now in fashion, what we are saying is that the term 'this' in the above proposition has to be *operationally defined* if the proposition is to be meaningful. Let us proceed to do this by translating the proposition to mean "at time t and place p a certain object O is red." (Of course this reformulation of the proposition is still not all that may be desired in the way of operational clarity and determinateness. The phrase "object O is red" needs further attention if the entire proposition is to be as explicit as one might wish to make it.)

Assuming our proposition does clearly establish the conditions included and those excluded when something is asserted to possess a certain characteristic, it is seen that these propositions are of two kinds. For in the above quotation, Dewey indicates that these propositions may be either the result of operations performed, or predictions of events that will occur when certain operations are performed. He gives as an example the proposition "this is soft," saying that it "means that *it* yields easily to pressure and will not cause most other things to yields when applied to them." [15] The proposition may, then, be the result of operations which serve as evidence for the assertion "this is soft." Or "this is soft" may be a prediction that *if* certain operations be performed they will reveal *this* to be soft. Obviously there is an important difference in the status of the proposition "this is soft." It is either a substantial assertion or a prediction; and the particular status which "this is soft" has is unknown, as it stands, unless some explicit qualification is added which states whether the proposition is the outcome of an investigation or a prediction of an occurrence to come. So when Dewey tells us that these propositions "represent the first stage in the *determination of a problem;* they supply a datum which, when combined with other data" *may* indicate the sort of problem and evidence a particular inquiry will be concerned with,[16] he would seem to be speaking of those propositions of the sort which can be said to indicate the "facts of the case." And as such, it should be observed, the propositions have the status of substantiated propositions, not predictions to be substantiated. For any particular empirical inquiry in seeking to arrive at some solution of a problem is going to have to make statements or propositions which are intended to be reports of certain facts or empirical events which have some bearing on the problem being inquired into. Supposing, for some reason, one wanted to determine how many men, attending a certain social gathering, are wearing red ties. One relevant fact of the case would be the statement "there are forty men present in this gathering at this time." One may then begin to gather other facts, making observations of each of the forty men. Suppose there are some men wearing red ties. When our inquirer observes these men, he states as a fact relevant to the outcome of his inquiry "this man is wearing a red tie." One may agree with Dewey that the proposition may *mean,* "if one performs certain operations of observations, etc., he will find this man possessing the characteristic asserted by the statement 'this man is wearing a red tie.' " The *meaning* of the proposition may have this predictive character, but the *status* of the proposition in an inquiry is not such that the proposition itself is a prediction, but rather a statement of fact, which as a statement of fact, has been made *after* certain operations of observation have been performed.

If particular propositions are to be defined or described as such, in the light of their function in actual inquiries as determining a problem and supplying the data and evidence of inquiries, it would seem more accurate to define them as propositions which are the results of operations performed and not, as Dewey allows, propositions which are predictions of results when certain operations are performed. This latter kind of proposition is most certainly important in empirical procedure, but they cannot, we have tried to suggest, be regarded as particular propositions, when particular propositions are assigned the specific role in inquiries which Dewey has given them.

We should also notice in connection with Dewey's discussion of particular propositions that the meaning of "particularity," as that term is employed in describing these propositions, is not entirely clear. Dewey says: ". . . the proposition is particular not because it applies to a singular but because the qualification is of *something taking place at a definite here and now, or is of an immediate change.*" [16] This means that any proposition which specifies temporal-spatial conditions is a particular proposition. But it is often convenient to distinguish a proposition of the sort: (1) "there is a red object in place p_1 at time t_1." from one asserting (2) "every object is red in p_1 at t_1." The distinction is exhibited in most explicit form when an adequat symbolization of these two propositions is constructed. (Very roughly, there is a formal difference being made between the statements "there is an x and x has the property P" where P means being red at p_1 and t_1, and "for every x, if x is an object, x has the property P.") Dewey writes "the logical import of a 'particular' is determined by the strictly limited local and temporal occurrence of the quality in question." [16] But there is obviously an important *empirical* difference between these statements. The first can be verified by finding one instance of a red object at p_1 and t_1. The second requires either an exhaustive observation of every object at p_1 and t_1, or can be refuted by finding one non-red object at p_1 and t_1. And of course if (2) should be found true, then (1) is true. And if (1) is found false, then no inquiry into (2) is required because it is also false. There are other consequences that elementary logic shows to follow from certain features of these propositions which here we can ignore. The point is that there *is* a distinction to be made between (1) and (2), and one wonders how valuable Dewey's own classification of particular propositions is, when both (1) and (2) are included under the heading of particular propositions. Dewey is as aware as any one else that there is a difference between (1) and (2); the objection is, however, that he seems to have neglected giving an account of this distinction where, presumably, it would most be expected, namely in describing the different kinds of propositions which are employed, and upon which successful inquiry depends.

One last difficulty may be mentioned as arising in the account of particular propositions. Dewey speaks of these propositions as referring to things "taking place" at a definite time and place. Again he speaks of them as about "a change that has occurred or is about to occurr." [17] And his examples are all of the sort "this is soft," "it is bright," "this is red," etc. In each case something is being predicated of something else, a "thing" is being asserted to possess a certain quality or characteristic. Since he has said that particular propositions are such because they designate something happening at a definite time and place, we may note that this feature, along with each of the above examples of such propositions, gives them the form of "x possesses the property P at t_1 and p_1." One is inclined to suppose that particular propositions have three features making them up: namely, 1) an x; 2) having the property P; 3) at a t_1 and p_1. One wonders, however, why Dewey has not mentioned propositions of the sort "red at t_1 and p_1" which, in another sense of the word 'particular' are very often said to stand as examples of the kind of particular propositions employed in empirical investigations. Obviously, "red at t_1 and p_1" is not the same as asserting "*this* is red at t_1 and p_1." For when the word 'this' is specified as designating a certain property—say a table—then "red at t_1 and p_1" may be true while "this (i.e. table) is red at t_1 and p_1 may be false. In the first case the simple fact of red at a time and place is asserted; in the second case something additional has been said. And though it may be true that red is at t_1 and p_1, it may not be true that what is red at t_1 and p_1 is a table.

Suppose, in the light of what has already been said about

the indeterminateness of empirical propositions having terms like "this," we define "this" to mean a specified object, say a certain table designated as table T. Then the latter proposition reads: "T is red at t_1 and p_1." But it is evident this this proposition itself is true or substantiated only in virtue of certain empirical operations. And these operations would include: a) determining if T was at t_1 and p_1; and b) determining if at t_1 and p_1 the quality of redness was present. The point involved here is that the proposition "this is red at t_1 and p_1" though it be a particular proposition in Dewey's sense, is itself, on analysis, shown to be a compound proposition made up of the two constituents: a) "T is at t_1 and p_1" and, b) "red at t_1 and p_1."

It can be shown that each one of Dewey's examples of particular propositions are, on analysis, compounded of these simpler, or less general (in the sense that they assert less) propositions. For we noticed that in the case of those propositions Dewey mentions, three features were involved in them and in what they were asserting. But in the proposition to which I am now drawing attention, only one feature is asserted; namely: red at t_1 and p_1. It is to be regretted, therefore, that Dewey does not mention these less general propositions under the heading of particular propositions. For these propositions, it is also held, are of some considerable importance, not only in specific inquiries, but in the accounts given of the various kinds of propositions employed in empirical inquiries. I should add, however, by way of avoiding possible misunderstandings, that the acceptance of the view concerning the nature of these "simple" propositions, does not of itself commit one to the position which is often associated with it, that the world is made up of "atomic facts" and the way the world is to be known is by arranging basic (or atomic) propositions in a kind of one-to-one correspondence with the neat facts of the world.

We have been concerned so far with Dewey's account of particular propositions. I have ventured to some extent a criticism of this account. Because Dewey's formulation of particular existential propositions departs considerably from what is normally understood by propositions of this sort, it is bound to appear new and somewhat strange. So important to any account of the procedural characteristics of empirical inquiries is the role of particular existential propositions, that the above discussion has dealt with issues concerning how these propositions are formulated (their operational formulation), their status in inquiries (as statements of the facts of the case), their distinction from other propositions (such as universal propositions), and the occurrence of "simple" particular propositions.

If this discussion has been substantially correct, we may, in summary, conclude as follows: 1) In his examples of particular propositions, Dewey has failed to offer propositions which can be regarded, as they are formulated, to assert anything definite; they are operationally indeterminate and as such cannot be regarded as statements having definite empirical significance. 2) Dewey's statement that particular propositions may be either already substantiated or predictions to be substantiated, goes against actual procedure. For statements reporting the data and evidential facts of inquiry must be taken as such and not as predictions; if the outcome of an inquiry is to be warranted (even if it is a prediction to be later verified) it must proceed from statements of some facts as evidence, which are not themselves to be verified, but which must constitute the grounds, the present conditions, for arriving at conclusions. 3) To regard "particular" statements simply as those which contain definite mention of time and place, fails to provide adequate grounds for distinguishing propositions asserting something about individuals at a time and place, and propositions asserting something to be the case about classes or entire collections of individuals at a time and place. 4) Lastly, the examples Dewey offers of particular propositions, are propositions which are compounded of simpler propositions. Each of the propositions stated by Dewey can be analyzed into two or more constituent propositions. Analysis may reveal this, but in the actual operations determining a proposition such as "this table is red" to be the case, there is an implicit separation and testing of the constituents of the proposition before it, as a whole, can be determined. That is, "this table is red" involves operations determining "this" to be a table at a time and place, and red to be observed at that time and place, etc. It might be suggested then, that not only do these constituent propositions deserve attention, but that they are possibly rightly regarded as "basic" in the sense that they singly, or in compounded forms, make up the class of propositions which can be called existential and particular.

Enough has been said concerning the above important class of propositions which Dewey discusses. His further account of other kinds of propositions is in general less perplexing and has, with one exception, close, if not direct, relations with distinctions already familiar in logical theory. Therefore we need not concern ourselves here with analysis of the various other sub-classes of propositions which he has listed. The exception is Dewey's formulation of universal and generic propositions. These are original contributions to logical theory and Dewey seems to place not a little emphasis on their importance. I will now turn, for this reason, to a discussion of these propositions.

B. UNIVERSAL PROPOSITIONS

Of universal and generic propositions, Dewey writes: "Universals and generics bear the same relation to each other in inquiry that material and procedural means sustain to each other in institution of judgment." [18] As such these propositions are obviously of crucial importance to inquiry, since, in a general sense, they serve to mark the two fundamental activities or functions that go on and they set the conditions for judgment and warranted conclusions of inquiry. We want to determine, then, what these propositions are, i.e., what are their distinguishing features? And secondly, we want to understand the place of these propositions in logical theory. Dewey says that universal propositions "are formulations of possible ways or modes of acting or operating." [19] These propositions, it seems, are "required for control of a way of acting that effects discrimination and ordering of existential material in its function as evidential data." [19] Again: "the existential basis of a universal proposition is a *mode of action* . . . it is not, however, *merely* a formulation as serves to direct the operations by means of which existential material is discriminated and related (ordered) so that it functions as the ground for warranted inferential conclusions . . . Through symbolization of propositional formulation they represent *possible* ways of action." [20]

Generic propositions, as distinguished from the above, are contingent and have existential reference about kinds (i.e., to the relating traits of existants in space and time.) "Every proposition that involves the conception of a kind is based upon a set of related traits or characteristics that are the necessary and sufficient conditions of describing a specified kind. These traits are selectively discriminated by observation out of the total perceived field." [21] Again, "the adequate grounding of such a proposition demands, accordingly, that related but excluded kinds be determinately established. This condition is satisfied when (1) an inclusive kind is determined, and (2) when the differentia are ascertained which exclusively mark out included kinds from one another:—in other words, a set of conjoined affirmations-negations." [22]

It is clear that since the logical form of these propositions may be identical, they cannot be distinguished by inspection of the statements in which they are formulated, but only by the reference such formulations have to the context of a particular inquiry, and to the specific operation or function in that inquiry which serve as the basis for distinguishing one proposition from another. This fact, let us observe, creates a condition which either drastically limits the freedom with which symbolization can usually be employed in the formalization of logic (since Dewey makes fundamental distinctions in meaning between propositions having the same logical form) or immensely complicates that symbolization to cover these non-formalized differences. Dewey gives an example of the proposition "All men are mortal." If this proposition is universal, he says, it asserts "a necessary interrelation of the characters *being* human and *being* mortal." It means, in this case, "If anything is human, *then* it is mortal." On the other hand, this proposition may be generic. Then it has a spatio-temporal import, subject to the contingencies of existence and matters of fact. In this latter sense, the proposition means: "All men have died or will die." [23]

Now logical theory, Dewey says, has suffered to date by failing to distinguish this difference in meaning. An account of the procedure of inquiry is piecemeal and incomplete if it fails to include these two types of propositions representing two distinct features within the act of inquiring. Whether or not we acquiesce to all this, it must be admitted that it is very difficult to determine in any precise way which does justice to the importance Dewey claims for them, just what these propositions are and the grounds on which distinctions are made between them. For instance, in one place Dewey tells us: "a universal hypothetical has the form of a definition in its logical sense." [24] In places he is concerned to show "the dependence of propositions about kinds upon the *definition* provided by universal hypothetical propositions." [25] Do these statements asserting universal propositions to be definitory in character, allow us to identify them with the analytic propositions of contemporary logical theory?[25] One is tempted to suppose this to be the case, for in addition to the above, Dewey has said his universal propositions "in their *necessary* interrelation . . . present the analysis of a conception into its integral and exhaustive contents." [26] In speaking of these propositions as having the function of definitions, and of asserting necessary relations between its constituent parts, the term "necessary" lends force to the consideration of these propositions as being analytic in nature. However great the temptation (and the desire for clarity and understanding urges this identification) to call Dewey's universal propositions the familiar analytic propositions wearing a strange disguise, this cannot be done. Not, at least, without doing violence in turn to what analytic propositions are commonly understood to mean. For Dewey tells us that universal propositions in formulating possible modes of action are themselves tested by their force and relevance in the determination of an inquiry.[27] Whereas analytic propositions are true by virtue of their form alone, of his universal propositions Dewey says "proof is effected by (1) the formulation of the idea suggested in a hypothetical proposition, and (2) by the transformation of data into a unified situation through execution of the operations presented by the hypothetical as a rule of action." [27]

But one is left to wonder what Dewey means by saying universal propositions assert *necessary* connections, or orders in the operation of selecting and discriminating materials for inquiry. And does he mean by saying that they state the *possible* modes of action, that such propositions state every possible operation in the logical sense of possible, where only operations which are self-contradictory in some way would be excluded? Presumably not; and apparently he doesn't mean "possible" in the physical sense of asserting that the proposition states every mode of operation compatible with, or not defying the laws of physics and the facts of the world. Apparently the possible modes of action or operating, that these propositions formulate are those relative to a certain context; that context being one which is disturbed and in which inquiry is going on. For, we may remember, these propositions "serve to direct the operations by means of which existential material is selectively discriminated and related (ordered) so that it functions as the ground for warranted inferential assertions." If one wished to hold Dewey to a strict interpretation of this passage, it would seem that a universal proposition *is* a universal proposition only when it conforms to this requirements. For the above passage (which I have quoted at length in a previous paragraph) discusses the nature of these propositions and stands, presumably, as a definition of them, or at least a statement of those of their characteristics by which they may be defined. As a consequence, we not only never know from a given statement alone whether it is a universal or generic proposition but only after a context of inquiry specifies it, we also never know whether a universal proposition *is such* until an inquiry is concluded. For supposing one takes one of these formulations of modes of acting. One never knows that the particular formulation at hand of a mode of acting as a hypothetical proposition will, on execution, result in a "transformation of data into a unified situation through execution of the operations presented by the hypothetical as a rule of action." This is only known *after* the execution of this mode of action. If, after trying the mode of action out, it results in ordering and relating existential material so that it serves as the ground for warranted inferential assertion, then we know we have a universal proposition. Supposing, however, this mode of action fails to achieve the above result. What can we then say? There are two possible answers: a) the proposition is not a universal proposition, since it has failed as a mode of action to achieve the above results required of such propositions. This would be tantamount to defining universal propositions as only those that do so achieve these desired results. The consequences are not fortunate. For we are then committed to the view that we never know in a specific inquiry, whether or not universal propositions are being employed at all, until some mode of action achieves certain results. Then miraculously a universal proposition is born. Consequently, the very purpose for introducing the notion of universal propositions as explanatory ideas for the description of what occurs in inquiries has been defeated. Some new terminology would have to be introduced by way of explaining what these notions or modes of acting were before they suddenly became universal propositions. More generally this view means we do not know what our instruments are, or how to recognize them, until after they have been successfully employed. b) The other possible answer to the above question is to say that a mode of acting which fails to achieve desired results is nonetheless a universal proposition, but one which has led us astray. We suspect this would be Dewey's answer, though he fails to make mention of such cases of universal propositions. Hence his discussion of the nature of such propositions is incomplete, for it does not account for unsatisfactory (I avoid the term "false" here for reasons soon to be made evident) universal propositions.

The difficulty here can be stated as follows. Universal propositions are formulations of possible modes of action; they facilitate inquiry in virtue of their function in ordering and discriminating various data, etc. Now, be it noted, it is the propositions which indicate (or first instigate) these modes of action. Now let us designate some specific universal proposition as P. P has the properties or characteristics and performs the function already discussed. The query may then be put as follows. In a particular inquiry, how is it possible to formulate P, or even recognize the formulation to be P, until after an operation (which P purports to formulate) has already been performed? For P as it is formulated cannot be distinguished in its formulation (i.e., as a statement or verbal formulation) from other kinds of propositions (e.g., generic propositions). So we only know that a given formulation *is* P, after the operations that proposition formulates have been performed. As a result of those operations we can then designate that formulation to be P or not to be P. But this begs the question; for it assumes we somehow know what operations to perform in virtue of which P can (or cannot) be designated and recognized. And certainly P is going to be of little value instrumentally, in indicating modes of action, if those indicated operations have first to be performed before we can know or recognize P. Suppose P be "all men are mortal." Dewey tells us this can be either a universal or generic proposition. How does one decide this in inquiry? Perhaps on the basis of some relation of P to other propositions; though I am at a loss to state this relation. But then we are merely taken back to other prior propositions and the above-stated difficulty remains only to be repeated. A way out of this difficulty, I tentatively suggest, is that certain minimum conditions or requirements be designated for the formulation of P. If the formulation of P could be accomplished in a fashion which, as a formulation, would distinguish P from other propositions, the necessary conditions for P would be established, so that in inquiries propositions of the kind P could at least be initially recognized, and as such, would prescribe specific kinds of operations to be performed. I shall not venture further to state what these requirements might be. But one can say that they must at least be such that a proposition of the sort "all men are mortal" *cannot* solely, in virtue of its formulation alone, be taken *either* as a universal or as some other kind of proposition. The requirements for the formulation of universal propositions would have to be such as not to make such identification of formulations possible.

But a difficulty still remains. Let us suppose that these propositions guide the ordering and transformation of data into a unified situation by means of formulated possible modes of action or fail to achieve this end. Again we only know if the proposition achieves or fails of this end *after* the operation it supposedly prescribes has been carried out. So again we only know if it *is* a universal proposition after we have already performed the functions it formulates. The instrumental or efficacious value of universal propositions for inquiry is thus unclear. The difficulty here, and it has bearing on Dewey's whole theory of propositions, is located in the apparent fact that Dewey defines or describes universal propositions in terms of the functions they perform in such a way that: a) their meaning or defined characteristics, or features that enable us to recognize them; b) their function or role in inquiry; and c) the manner in which they are determined satisfactory or unsatisfactory (their verification), are each hardly distinguishable. Now supposing no problems arise if a) and b) are identified, should a) and b) be indistinguishable from c) then the above difficulties arise. For it then results that we can only recognize a universal proposition by determining whether or not it is satisfactory i.e., by actually attempting to verify it. Hence the value for logical theory of this conception of universal propositions is called into question.

If universal propositions are not analytic, nor necessary in the sense of being true by virtue of their form alone, yet at the same time function (partially, at least) as definitions, what are they? Let us consider several examples Dewey gives us of these propositions. These propositions, he says, take the form: "*if* certain contents, then necessarily certain other contents." [28] Ignoring for the present those questions which occur with Dewey's use of the term 'necessarily,' we may consider what Dewey means when he says of these propositions, that the relation of antecedent and consequence is to be understood in a purely logical, not existential, sense. Hence the statement, "if I first do this, then certain consequences may be anticipated to follow," is not a universal proposition. The relation between clauses "is one of temporal priority and consequence." [28] But the proposition, "if an act of trespassing, then liability to penalty," Dewey says, is an example where the relation of terms in the antecedent and consequent "is non-temporal and non-existential." [28] One wonders what the reasons are for preferring the if-then form, if that form is to indicate a logical connection. For the connective "if-then" is but one of a number of connectives, and is itself derivable from certain other connectives (e.g., "if a then b," is derivable, on one definition of "if-then," from "either not a or b." Indeed, those familiar with the Peirce-Sheffer stroke function know that all of the binary connectives can be defined by one primitive notion.) The selection of various connective forms is but a matter of symbolic convenience. Since Dewey is not concerned with symbolization the preference for the form "if-then" remains unexplained. But let us turn to other examples he gives of these propositions. "When it is said," Dewey points out, " 'If a plane figure is a triangle, then the sum of its three interior angles is equal to two right angles,' not only is the *relation* non-existential, but the contents are free from any prescribed existential reference even of the most indirect sort."[28] And of this example, Dewey adds: "in such a proposition there is not even a semblance of antecedent and consequent even in a logical sense." [29] Now the question that obviously arises is: is this example adduced as an illustration of a universal proposition? If the answer is yes, then we have a proposition which, Dewey tells us, does not have "even a semblance of antecedent and consequent even in a logical sense." And it certainly has no semblance of antecedent and consequent in an existential sense. But how then are we to account for the fact that Dewey has already told us that universal propositions are expressed in an *if-then* form which means "if certain contents, then necessarily certain other contents"? What does this statement mean if in some universal propositions "there is not even a semblance of antecedent and consequent even in a logical sense"? And further, if the above *is* an example of a universal proposition, whose "contents are free from any prescribed existential reference even of the most indirect sort" how can we reconcile this fact with Dewey's statement that a "universal proposition prescribes the conditions to be *satisfied by existential material...*" [30] It is difficult to see how a proposition whose contents, we are told, "are free from any prescribed existential reference even of the most indirect sort" can at the same time be classified as one among those whose formulation "is *such* a formulation as serves to direct the operations by means of which existential material is selectively discriminated and related (ordered) so that it functions as the ground for warranted inferential conclusions."

It would hardly do to answer that the above mathematical example was not intended as an illustration of a universal proposition. The context of Dewey's discussion would indicate this latter view to be mistaken. For he says of those paragraphs in which the example is to be found, that they are intended to show what is meant by the functional character of universal propositions. [31] And it is also from this same example (which would indicate that he regards it to be an example of a universal proposition) that he draws the conclusion: "a universal hypothetical proposition has the form of a definition in its logical sense." [31] Hence it would certainly seem that Dewey does intend the above mathematical proposition to be an example of a universal proposition. And consequently the question still remains as to how a proposition which is admittedly "free from any prescribed existential reference even of the most indirect sort" can at the same time be regarded to "direct the operations by means of which existential material is selectively discriminated and related (ordered) so that it functions as the ground for warranted inferential conclusions."

There is one sense in which a definition in a mathematical system, or a definition of a notion employed in a certain branch of mathematics can be said to "direct the operations by means of which existential material is selectively related (ordered) . . . etc.," or, "prescribes the conditions to be satisfied by existential material." This sense is (roughly) as follows: a certain inquiry concerned to settle some disturbed situation, may find that it is necessary, or at least very much more convenient, to employ mathematics as an instrument in the calculations required in reaching some conclusion. And, it might be argued, mathematics cannot be employed or even be available if the mathematics required as an instrument in this inquiry has not itself been systematized, i.e., if it has no explicit apparatus including denitions, rules governing use of symbols, theorems, etc. Hence in an inquiry making use of mathematics, use is also being made of (say) the definitions and theorems which, in part, make up that system of mathematics. So if mathematics is being employed in the inquiry, and if some definition is part of that system of mathematics, and if inquiries are concerned with existential material, then a definition in the mathematical system might be said to help "direct the operations by means of which existential material is selectively ordered..." or "prescribes the conditions to be satisfied by existential material." In this sense, perhaps, one might wish to say that a notion which is itself "free from any existential reference even of the most indirect sort" can be regarded to "provide the conditions to be satisfied by existential material." In some obvious fashion this may be true; but I think it unlikely that Dewey could wish to rest his discussion of universal propositions, and claim that discussion to be significant, on such meagre ground. For it may be true, but it is certainly trivial to claim that in iquirying as to whether or not there are two apples in the next room, Frege's definition of number is instrumental in providing "the conditions to be satisfied by existential material" and thereby helping to provide the ground for warranted conclusions.

Leaving the above difficulties and questions to stand as they are, let us consider one other example Dewey offers of a universal proposition. After stating that "a universal hypothetical proposition has the form of a definition in its logical sense" Dewey says: "thus the proposition 'If anything is a material body, it attracts other material bodies directly as its mass and indirectly as the square of the distance' may be read equally well in the linguistic form 'All material bodies etc.' It is a (partial) definition of *being* a material body. It expresses a condition which any observed thing must satisfy if the property *'material'* is groundedly applicable to it." [31] In a later passage Dewey points out that while the proposition employs in its formulation certain abstract notions such as *mass, distance,* and *attraction,* the "proposition is framed with reference to the possibility of ultimate existential application" and "the contents are affected by that intent." [32] Consequently, such propositions may, when the facts indicate them to be inadequate, be either changed or abandoned for more appropriate formulations of the subject-matter under concern. They are subject, then, to change in the light of the accomplishments of progressive inquiries, and are contingent upon certain existential conditions for their status and acceptability. On the other hand, in propositions of mathematics, such as "2+2=4," "the interpretation to be put upon the contents is irrelevant to any material considerations whatever." [32] These propositions are thus free from any limitation of an existential sort. Because of these differences, Dewey indicates that a further distinction is necessary; these two examples demand that "*two* logical types of universal propositions must be distinguished." [33]

Since it is difficult to understand Dewey's distinction between universal and generic propositions, it becomes all the more obscure what this differences is when we are told that a further distinction must be made between universal propositions. Clearly there is a difference in the above two propositions. A difference usually stated in a rather precise way as the difference between *synthetic* and *analytic* propositions. But we have already noticed that this kind of a distinction cannot be made in the light of Dewey's remarks about the way in which universal propositions are tested and are determined to have an acceptable place in inquiry. As Professor Nagel has pointed out, [34] there is a serious question as to whether Dewey, in citing the Newtonian law of gravitation as an example of a universal proposition, is not doing violence to his own method by isolating a proposition from a specific context, and in turn blurring the distinction between universal and generic propositions. For there may be some cases of inquiries where this proposition is employed as a means of selecting and ordering specified traits and relationships of kinds observed in existential material and affording grounds for inference and further operations to be performed. Having this kind of a function, the proposition is generic and not universal. As a generic proposition, it is considerably more than a definition of how the term *'material'* is to be employed in a "groundedly applicable" way to observed things.

In displaying the difference between a proposition of physics and one of mathematics, Dewey seems to want to formulate this crucial distinction in terms of different kinds of necessary relations involving these propositions. He says "In . . . propositions (including all those of mathematical physics) the strictly mathematical phase resides in the necessary relation which *propositions* sustain one to another, not in their contents." [32] Whereas, speaking of mathematical propositions, he says: "this type of universal hypothetical proposition is therefore logically certifiable by formal relations, because formal relations determine also the terms of contents, the 'material,' as they cannot do in any universal proposition having ultimate existential application." [35] The difference then seems to be that some hypothetical universal propositions are such because of the necessary relation they bear to other such propositions. While some other hypothetical universal propositions are such because their content is determined formally or is necessarily related. This, I repeat, is what Dewey *seems* to mean, though I am by no means sure that this is what he does mean. But taking this distinction as it is, it is clear that it depends on what is meant by the term "necessary" if the distinction itself is to be meaningful. (I have already noted previously Dewey's unexplained use of "necessary"). Nowhere, as far as I can discover, does Dewey explicitly formulate and explain what he means by that term. Let us suppose, then, that it has the only meaning that would be relevant in the above context, that is, the usual meaning of "necessary" in contemporary logical theory. According to this usage, to say a proposition is necessary, is to say that it is formulated in such a way that a denial of it involves a violation of a rule of logic. Necessary, or necessarily true propositions are such that propositions denying them are not merely false but self-contradictory. Let us attempt to give examples of the above two types of universal propositions. The latter is relatively simple, if to say that its contents or terms involve a necessary relation is to mean propositions of the sort: "If this is a black crow, then this is black," or "If there are four people in this room then there are more then two people in this room." Here the contents of terms within the proposition bear a relation to one another which might be described as such that the proposition is itself a *necessary proposition*. (I preserve the hypothetical form here only because of Dewey's insistence that universal propositions take that form, though in the case of mathematical and all necessary propositions, that form is not only not required but is often an undesirably clumsy accruement.)

What about the other kind of hypothetical universal proposition which, Dewey says, is one because of "the necessary relation which propositions sustain one to another, not in their contents"? The contents of these propositions have some reference to, and are determined by, considerations of existential application. Suppose one takes Dewey's own example: "If anything is a material body, it attracts other material bodies directly as its mass and indirectly as the square of the distance." As it stands all we have is one proposition, and hence there is no example of necessary relations between propositions. Hence, we might add to the above: "If the books in my room are material, then they attract each other directly as their mass and indirectly as the square of their distance." It is evident that if the first proposition is true, then the second is also true. The second proposition being true in the sense that any proposition which is derived in accordance with the rules of logic, from a true premise, is true. And this seems to be the only possible sense in which one can say that the propositions are such that there is a "necessary relation which the propositions sustain one to another" and their contents are not necessarily related. That is, "being material" is not necessarily related to "attracting other material bodies directly as its mass . . . etc." For I can assert "this is material and it does not attract other bodies directly as its mass, etc." and not be asserting something self-contradictory.

If this be the sense in which some universal propositions are characterized as such, because they sustain a necessary relation one to another, it is evident that we are being told little or nothing of value about the characteristic features of certain universal hypothetical propositions. For any given proposition, one can always find some other proposition which is such that the two sustain a necessary relation to each other. And in the case of hypothetical propositions, given any proposition, e.g., "If anyone is a philosopher then he is mad," I can construct a proposition "If Smith is a philosopher then Smith is mad," and, as such, it might be said that there is a "necessary relation which the propositions sustain one to another."

But of course if that *is* the sense in which Dewey wishes to distinguish universal hypothetical propositions of the sort that appear in mathematical physics, from those in pure mathematics, it is obvious that to say that the first are such that there is a necessary relation which the propositions sustain one to another, while the second are such that the contents of the propositions are necessarily related, we are: 1) not being told very much; and 2) what we are being told, in part, goes against what Dewey tells us elsewhere.

This may be made sufficiently evident as follows: 1) To say that some universal propositions have the characteristic which Dewey says is that of a "necessary relation which the propositions sustain one to another" is to say nothing more than that some propositions are true by virtue of some relation they have to another proposition which is true. Or, more accurately: if a proposition P is true (or warrantably grounded etc.) and another proposition P_1 can be shown to be derived from P in accordance with the rules of logic, then we may say P_1 is true. P_1 being formally derivable from P, and P being true, it follows *necessarily* that P_1 is true. Hence to say some proposition sustain necessary relations to one another, means that some propositions are formally derivable or deducible from others. And this fact may be significant in an account of the procedures involved in inquiry. But this fact is hardly sufficient to tell us anything significant about those characteristics, features, or kinds of propositions that have this above relation to other propositions. The fact of the relation tells us nothing about the propositions related; nor are we any more clear about what hypothetical universal propositions are. 2) It was mentioned above that when Dewey seemed to say that a proposition of mathematics asserted a necessary relation between the terms or content of that proposition, it was of the sort that may be called *necessary,* or a necessarily true proposition. This would give an unambiguous interpretation to Dewey's discussion of this class of universal propositions. However, such an interpretation cannot be given them; for it identifies them with what is known as analytic propositions, and I have already shown in previous passages why this identification goes against certain significant features of Dewey's discussion of the function and test of universal propositions.

We are forced to conclude, for the reasons I have attempted to make sufficiently clear in the above discussion, that in Dewey's discussion and formulation of universal propositions it is neither evident what universal propositions are, nor, consequently, how they are to be distinguished from other kinds of propositions. It may be noticed that I have dealt only with issues concerning universal propositions and have said little or nothing about generic propositions. This neglect of the latter is due not primarily because Dewey's discussion of them is any more clear, but to the fact that Dewey says: "No grounded generic proposition can be formed save as they are products of the performance of operations indicated as possible by universal propositions." [36] Certainly then, an understanding of universal propositions is necessary if we are to completely understand Dewey's generic kind. And since an understanding of universal propositions is almost a necessary condition for clearly understanding Dewey's entire account of universal and generic proposition, I have thought it best to devote attention to those most perplexing and troublesome features of that account concerning what is there said about universal propositions. Until those initial difficulties have been cleared up, Dewey's entire account of universal and generic propositions remains an obscure and puzzling hypothesis, the value of which has yet to be determined.

C. A SUGGESTED INTERPRETATION OF GENERIC
AND UNIVERSAL PROPOSITIONS

Let us end, however, on a somewhat more positive note than this. Suppose we consider briefly at least some kind of propositions involved in most inquiries. There are going to be certain propositions whose status is almost, if not entirely, dependent on empirical material. Any such proposition would be those particular propositions already discussed. Also included among this first general group may be propositions asserting some particular existential event to have membership in a class of events: a particular object may be asserted to be an acorn. And a more general proposition may assert the class of all acorns to be a member of a larger class of all those classes of tree-producing seeds, etc. To these propositions asserting general characteristics or traits holding among existential things, Dewey's generic propositions seem to be applicable. These propositions would not only have reference to empirical events, to characteristics by which events can be distinguished and classified, but enable inference to events not observable. Such propositions would be related to existential events, but not directly dependent on any particular event in the sense that particular propositions are. If these are Dewey's generic propositions, it is to be noted that their acceptance or rejection does not seriously effect the theoretical structure of the sciences, but only involves changes in the status of the conclusions of inquiries having a related place, but not a basic position, in the structure of a science.

Distinguished from any of the aforementioned propositions, however, are those which have achieved such a fundamental place in the body of one or more sciences, covering both a wide range of empirical affairs and providing a rich source for deductive consequences, that for the purposes of particular inquiries they have the status of an assumed finality. That is, the conclusions of particular inquiries will be reached and appraised with reference to the assumed validity of these fundamental propositions. They have less direct existential import than those conclusions derived from them and the particular inquiries which they guide; but their place in all inquiries is such that they are a necessary condition for advanced and significant inquiry. Now, at the same time, there are other more formal but no less significant propositions, involved in any inquiry which function as leading principles, warranting the reasoning from certain premises to some conclusion. Peirce says: "It is the essence of reasoning that the reasoner should proceed, and should be conscious of proceeding, according to a general habit, or method, which he holds would either . . . always lead to the truth, providing the premises were true; or, consistently adhered to, would eventually approximate indefinitely to the truth . . . The effect of this habit or method could be stated in a proposition of which the antecedent should describe all possible premises upon which it could operate, while the consequent should describe how the conclusion to which it would lead would be determinately related to those premises. Such a proposition is called the 'leading principle' of the reasoning." [37] So, for example, in some inquiry certain propositions are going to be assumed as a basis upon which that inquiry can proceed. Depending on the nature of the inquiry, either initially, or at some intermediate stage before a conclusion is reached, it will be employing certain propositions which lead the inquiry (in the sense that "if this proposition, then such and such results are to be expected") and serve as a means of appraising certain results arrived at. Such a proposition, for example Newton's law of gravitation, may have this function in an inquiry. And this kind of proposition, I have just suggested, may be one kind of universal proposition in Dewey's account; it has indirect existential import and may be a crucial assumption for certain inquiries. Let us designate this proposition, having a place in some particular inquiry, as P. The inquiry being supposed here, will employ P in this manner: propositions of the form "If P then such and such consequences are to be expected" will be entertained. Some empirical material may then be determined to fall under the requirements of the consequences deductively arrived at from P. Then the proposition occurs: "This material possesses the features which P asserted it should possess." An important proposition; not so much because P is confirmed in one instance but because since P is assumed true, the operation of the inquiry show it, so far, to be not unwarranted. If, on the other hand, the operations of the inquiry disclose some material which should possess characteristics as asserted by P, but in fact do not, then (again assuming P to be true) the inquiry is shown to be running amiss and is in need of correction.

As it stands, this account of certain kinds of propositions employed in an inquiry is seriously inadequate. For it is evident that P (as a law or theory) yields no deductive consequences for an inquiry unless certain initial conditions are provided, which, along with P, enable relevant deductions to be obtained. Thus if P asserts "if X then Y" (X and Y being here meant to stand for the properties asserted in the Newtonian law of gravitation) nothing of particular value for an inquiry can be obtained from P until the initial proposition asserting conditions meeting the requirements for X is established. Then Y can be asserted to follow. So we may have the propositions: (1) "if X then Y;" (2) "conditions satisfying the requirements set by X are present"; (3) "hence conditions asserted by Y must be also present." The determination of (2) is an empirical affair involving other propositions of particular, singular, or generic sort, or perhaps all of these kinds.

Rules of logic permit the inference that: if (If X then Y, and X) then Y. But the rules of logic do not provide for determining if their application to the specific reasoning material of some inquiry is relevant or adequate. That is, one may know the rules for making valid infernces, yet the application of that knowledge to some particular problem is not provided for among the rules of logic. In most inquiries the reasoning may involve more complicated inferences, and more consequences, than in the above argument. There may be more than one premise of the sort, If X then Y, and there may be a number of conclusions.

Thus it may often be quite necessary and valuable to order the various premises and possible conclusions; this ordering will be accomplished by propositions and after sheering away the most unlikely possibilities to meet the demands of the problem of that inquiry, the various premises may be stated along with the possible conclusions in one proposition which can be called a "leading principle."

The leading principle states the premises with which the inquiry at any one stage may wish to employ and expresses in its consequent the results which would be expected to follow if these premises were employed.

It is, of course, of the nature of the particular inquiry in question as to whether a particular leading principle is relevant and whether or not it assists the inquiry in reaching a conclusion. But two features of the leading principle are worth mentioning. First, as a proposition, it is not determined for its truth or falsehood by existential reference; it asserts that from certain premises certain conclusions are to be obtained. Its truth, in all cases, will depend on whether or not from a set of stated premises a set of stated conclusions do follow. Its truth, then, depends on formal considerations; as to if it is the case by the rules of logic that the stated conclusions are the deductive consequences of the stated premises. Secondly, the leading principle states "a mode of action" or "possible ways or modes of acting or operating" (to use Dewey's language) for an inquiry. It indicates what consequences may be expected, if certain premises are assumed.

The proposition expressing a leading principle, I suggest, may be the other kind of hypothetical universal proposition with which Dewey is concerned. His universal propositions would then be of the sort that are found as laws or theories in a science and the leading principles which combine propositions of this first kind with the material of specific inquiries and hence indicate possible directions which that inquiry may take. If these are the two kinds of universal propositions, the first having existential bearing, but directing and facilitating inquiry nonetheless significantly, they are well worth considering in any account of the nature of inquiries. Especially is this true of the notion of propositions as leading principles, since very little mention is to be found of them in most accounts of empirical inquiries. Dewey's discussion, in spite of its opaque character, has the merit of drawing our attention to these usually neglected, yet most important matters. Much of what Dewey says about his universal propositions appears to describe one or the other of these two kinds which I have dealt with here. The difficulties clustering around his statements that universal propositions, relate *necessary characters,* and are free from existential reference yet have existential import, might, when that language is clarified, apply to those propositions here called "leading principles."

Yet in spite of these suggested meanings to Dewey's account of universal propositions I cannot feel certain that I have clarified matters very much. For, as I have already observed, Dewey might be proposing a method of proving the force and relevance of all universal propositions in a manner which partially, if not wholly, excludes these leading principle propositions.[38] For it may be that their relevance is determined by how they "prescribe conditions to be satisfied by existential material" but the force or status (or truth) of these leading principles is a matter of logic alone. And further, we cannot overlook the fact that Dewey holds that the propositions of mathematics are also universal propositions. But the propositions of mathematics are analytic. They are thus very different from the propositions I have been discussing. It is evident, therefore, that this entire discussion by way of suggesting what Dewey's universal propositions might be, even were it entirely correct, must consequently be considered only partially complete. There are very good reasons for thinking that the propositions of mathematics are in important respects different from the other propositions Dewey wishes to call universal propositions. Until Dewey clarifies his own position on this and related matters his own account of universal propositions must be regarded as incomplete and remain a view to which no definite appraisal can finally be given.

D. THE GENERAL FEATURE OF DEWEY'S THEORY OF
   PROPOSITIONS: AN APPRAISAL

We have seen that there are certain difficulties to be met in Dewey's account of proposition: specifically, difficulties to be found in his presentation of the notions of particular and universal propositions. I want to turn now to a more general feature of Dewey's theory of propositions as such. Perhaps the most striking innovation of Dewey's entire theory is that propositions are not to be regarded as true or false. It is to this underlying feature of his whole account of the nature of propositions and their functions in inquiry that I wish now, in what follows, to give some attention.

As has already been mentioned, Dewey is concerned to make a sharp distinction between propositions as intermediate features within inquiry and judgment which is the outcome or conclusive phase of inquiry. His point may bear repeating here. He says "Judgment may be identified as the settled outcome of inquiry. It is concerned with the concluding objects that emerge from inquiry in their status of being *conclusive*. Judgment in this sense is distinguished from *propositions*. The content of the latter is intermediate and representative and is carried by symbols; while judgment, as finally made, has *direct* existential import. The terms *affirmation* and *assertion* are employed in current speech interchangeably. But there is a difference, which should have linguistic recognition, between the logical status of intermediate subject-matters that are for use in connection *with what they lead to as means,* and subject-matter which has been prepared to be final. I shall use *assertion* to designate the latter logical status and *affirmation* to name the former. . ." [39]

On this view, Dewey tells us, "propositions are what are affirmed but not asserted." [40] Propositions "are means, instrumentalities, since they are the operational agencies by which *beliefs* that have adequate grounds for acceptance are reached as *end* of inquiry."[40] In what follows I shall depart from Dewey's usage to this extent: I will use the terms "proposition" and "judgment" to refer to those intermediate and final subject-matters of inquiry which Dew-

ey has formulated. But I shall employ the term "assertion" to mean, roughly, that which is uttered or formulated
in language. Thus propositions are asserted as well as judgments. I do this to avoid possible confusion, for it is of
little apparent value to say some things are affirmed and
others asserted in inquiries when these terms are not themselves clearly distinguishable, and when what they are supposed to distinguish has already been distinguished by the
terms "proposition" and "judgment."

One other matter perhaps needs clarification before we
can proceed to the issue facing us. One may ask: if propositions are said to have an instrumental status within inquiry, to what are they instrumental? That is, if propositions are means, they are means to what? The answer occasionally given to this question is, propositions are instrumental or means to producing desired results. But this is
not a satisfactory answer unless it is understood what is to
be meant by "desired results." Since propositions are, according to Dewey, intermediate features in inquiry, they
do not produce the concluding stage of satisfying the unsettled or problematic situation. The "desired results"
which propositions can be said to produce is the stage of
grounded belief or judgment. And it is this latter stage in
turn, which leads to the conclusion of inquiry. Propositions, therefore, can be said to produce the conclusions to
inquiries only indirectly.

In holding that propositions have this instrumental character Dewey says: "the conclusion or end of inquiry has to
be demarcated from the intermediate means by which inquiry goes forward to a warranted or justified conclusion
that . . . the intermediate means are formulated in discourse, i.e., as propositions, and that as means they have
the properties appropriate to means (viz., relevancy and

efficacy-including economy) ."[41] As a result of this view it should be "clear that, according to it, truth and falsity are properties only of that subject-matter which is the *end,* the close of the inquiry by means of which it is reached. The distinction between true and false conclusions is determined by the character of the operational procedures through which propositions about data and propositions about inferential elements (meaning, ideas, hypotheses) are instituted." Hence, Dewey concludes, he "cannot imagine that one who says that such things as hammers, looms, chemical processes like dyeing, reduction of ores, when used as means, are marked by properties of fitness and efficacy (and the opposite) rather than by the properties of truth-falsity, will be thought to be saying anything that is not common-place." [41]

As far as I have been able to discover, this paragraph states in as concise and clear a fashion as any Dewey has written, his reasons for regarding propositions as neither true nor false. In his *Logic,* Dewey offers what is substantially the same argument. In what seems to be the main passage on this subject he writes: "The view most current at the present time is probably that which regards propositions as the unitary material of logical theories. Propositions upon this view have their defining property in the property of formal truth-falsity. According to the position here taken, propositions are to be differentiated and identified on the ground of the function of their contents as means, procedural and material, further distinctions of forms of propositions being instituted on the ground of the special ways in which their respective characteristic subject-matters function as means . . . But at this point it is pertinent to note that, since means as such are neither true nor false, truth-falsity is not a property of propositions. Means are either effective or ineffective; pertinent or irrelevant; wasteful or economical, the criterion for the difference being found in the consequences with which they are connected as means." [42] In the *Logic*, then, the same kind of reasons are offered for holding this view as those stated in the above paragraph. Consequently, I hope no injustice is being done, if, for the sake of clarity and convenience, I direct our discussion of Dewey's view primarily in the light of what he writes as quoted in the paragraph above. I shall suppose that paragraph to be an accurate representation of Dewey's position. It presents, in concentrated form, the main reasons (if not all of them) dispersed by Dewey in various isolated passages throughout the *Logic*. Also, for convenience, I will refer in the following, to this statement of Dewey's in the above paragraph, as "paragraph P." Paragraph P, I shall assume then, is an adequate formulation of Dewey's reasons for holding that proposition do not possess the properties of truth-falsity.

In considering the merits of the above view concerning the nature of propositions, certain points, of a serious and critical sort must be brought into the open. There are, we may observe, two general objections to be urged against this aspect of Dewey's notion of propositions. First, Dewey's interpretation of the function of propositions within inquiries does not of itself necessarily exclude the usual view that propositions are to be regarded as possessing the fundamental characteristic of being either true or false. That is, as I shall try to show, one can maintain the essential features of Dewey's discussion of the role of propositions in inquiry and at the same time not be forced to regard propositions as lacking any truth values. Secondly, there are independent reasons for wishing to preserve the truth value feature of propositions. If truth and falsehood are to be abolished as properties of propositions, a number of very serious and upsetting consequences occur, not only affecting logic, but empirical procedure as well. And these consequences ought to receive some attention from those who wish to propose and maintain such a view. That the foundations of logic and much of the analysis of empirical method are shaken by the notion that propositions are neither true nor false may be an unpleasant consequence, but this fact in itself is hardly a sufficient reason for dismissing the view which leads to such unhappy circumstances. But it makes it all the more important to consider how compelling and forceful the reasoning may be that wishes to reject the properties of truth and falsehood from propositions. Dewey is not alone, it might be noted, in proposing this revision in our understanding of the fundamental properties of propositions; but what I intend to say here will be concerned solely with his views and hence only indirectly with other views where they may coincide with Dewey's in the points discussed below.

The fundamental characteristic of propositions in Dewey's theory, it would seem, is their status as means in inquiries. Hence Dewey not infrequently compares propositions to tools of one kind or another which functions as the agents or things-by-which a job can be accomplished and completed. The comparison is enlightening when what is to be understood by propositions as means in an inquiry is being clarified and explained. Yet the fact that propositions are means, Dewey seems to think, necessitates in addition to what this might mean, the notion that propositions do not possess the property of being true or false. For the reasons already stated, this additional notion is of crucial importance and demands attention.

Attention may begin by noting that though propositions and tools may be significantly compared and found to have properties in common there are also significant differences to be taken into account. It is just at these points of difference that, I think, Dewey draws more than is warranted from the analogies and illustrations of propositions as "tools" in inquiries. Suppose one says with Dewey that, just as a hammer is a tool in the construction of a house and as a tool possesses the characteristics "of fitness and efficacy (and the opposite) ," so a proposition in inquiry possesses these characteristics. By way of this analogous character of hammers and propositions one may have illustrated with some clarity what is to be meant by saying that propositions are means, or instruments, in an inquiry, and also the further fact that, as means propositions possess the characteristics of means, i.e., "fitness and efficacy (and the opposite) ."

Now supposing this much to be evident and sufficiently reasonable. May we also reasonably go on to say that since hammers and tools (or means in general) are marked by the properties "of fitness and efficacy (and the opposite) " and are certainly not marked by the properties of truth-falsity, and since propositions are means, it is nothing more than commonplace to say that propositions are also not marked by the properties of truth-falsity? Without hesitation, I should answer this question in the negative. And though in this form, Dewey might also answer the question in the same way, the grounds for his argument that propositions are not true or false, as far as I can see, consists in concluding from the fact that since propositions and tools (hammers, looms, etc.) have certain features in common (viz., the characteristics possessed by all means) it follows that because e.g., a hammer is neither true nor false, that a proposition must be neither true nor false. Of course, Dewey never presents his view in this fashion; yet in those passages (e.g. paragraph P) where he says that by his theory propositions are not true nor false, the reason he gives may be detected to follow the above line of thought. The heart of that line of thought, I repeat, consists in identifying propositions as means to ends, and then showing that means are neither true nor false, but rather, fit, efficacious, efficient, relevant, etc. (and the opposite).

I need not also repeat that the analogy between propositions and hammers, looms, etc. is valuable when the notion of propositions as means and tools in inquiry is being explained. When the analogy is taken too literally it may lead one to overlook certain very important differences between tools as means or instruments for achieving certain ends and propositions as means or instruments in achieving the final phase of inquiry. These differences may be made clear when we consider what a proposition is. Propositions, as has been said, are "the necessary logical instrumentalities of reaching final warranted determination or judgment." [43] They are also to be described, however, as formulations, symboliations having reference to material or procedural features of an inquiry, Dewey says. He writes: "Only by means of symbolization (the peculiar differentia of propositions) can direct action be deferred until inquiry into conditions and procedures has been instituted." [43] When, therefore, propositions are said to be means or instruments it must not be forgotten that they are also formulations or symbolic features by which certain necessary parts of inquiries are carried on. This more or less obvious fact must be kept in mind when

Dewey further tells us: "Propositions . . . are, consequently, provisional, intermediate and instrumental." [43] Hammer, looms, and tools in general may also be provisional, intermediate and instrumental in the attainment of some ends. Yet they are not propositions.

Suppose some one should be inquiring into the problem of building a house in a region well provided with trees and having easy access to a lumber mill. He may decide provisionally that the most efficient means, as far as materials go, with which to build the house will be wood. In the course of this inquiry he may make use of the proposition: "hammers and nails are necessary for the construction of wooden houses." The proposition may be provisional, intermediate and instrumental in the inquiry and in reaching a conclusion to the inquiry. And hammers and nails may be intermediate and instrumental in building the house. In this respect both the proposition and hammers are means and instruments. Yet it is also the case that no house can ever be put together with propositions and no final determination or judgment can be arrived at by means of hammers. Examples of this point can be multiplied indefinitely. If I am lost in my hotel, I may formulate the proposition: "my room is somewhere down this corridor." The proposition doesn't get me any closer to my room, though it may assist me in calculating the actions I may have to take in order to find my room. In this case too, both the proposition and walking down the corridor may be means or instruments to my finding my room.

The point to be noticed is that *both* the act of walking down the corridor and the proposition "my room is somewhere down this corridor" are instruments or *means* in this particular inquiry. Since they are both instruments or means in the same inquiry, crucial distinctions between them may be momentarily unnoticed. When this happens the results are often absurd. If the two are not distinguished then, when I say "my room is somewhere down this corridor" (and the proposition happens to be true), I miraculously am transported to my room by formulating a proposition. It is evident that propositions and that which is formulated by propositions have to be distinguished. Whatever a proposition may be about, as a proposition, i.e., a piece of symbolism, it cannot be regarded as in any sense identical with that to which the proposition or symbolization refers. If this distinction be denied it follows that whenever one says "this table is red" what he utters has the quality of being red and the characteristics of tabularity. Ordinarily Dewey certainly would not fail to distinguish propositions from that which propositions are about, or symbolizations from that being symbolized. Yet I suspect that this distinction is blurred in Dewey's concern to emphasize that propositions and that which propositions are about are both instrumental or means in inquiries. When this distinction is blurred it is easily said that (as in the above) since walking down the corridor is an efficient or inefficient way to locate the room but certainly not an act possessing properties of truth-falsity, so the proposition "my room is somewhere down this corridor" being also an efficient or an inefficient instrument in this inquiry, also lacks the properties of truth-falsity. Yet in this case it is evident that the proposition speaks about, or formulates a state of affairs, which exists or does not exist. And it is the existence of this state of affairs and the formulation about it, which make up the conditions usually regarded as determining the truth or falsehood of that formulation.

If what I have been saying so far is not altogether

clear or convincing we may consider again Dewey's statement in paragraph P. He says that (a) ". . . hammers, looms, chemical processes like dyeing, reduction of ores, when used as means, are marked by properties of fitness and efficacy (and the opposite) rather than by the properties of truth-falsity. . ." And, we have seen since Dewey regards propositions in inquiries to be "used as means" he takes it to be a commonplace that it follows (b) that propositions will therefore be "marked by properties of fitness and efficacy (and the opposite) rather than by the properties of truth-falsity."

In considering these two statements (a) and (b), which seem to present the essential features of Dewey's argument that propositions are neither true nor false, I have been attempting to show that although (a) most certainly seems true, it by no means follows that (b) is also true. Now there are, of course, two possible ways in which someone might wish to maintain (b) to be true. We may call these (b_1) and (b_2). Since we are supposing (a) to be true, one way in which someone might wish to maintain (b) to be true is to maintain that (b) *follows* from (a) or is implied by (a) in the sense generally meant when it is said that a certain conclusion follows from, or is implied by, a certain premise. And it is in this respect, so far as I have been able to discover, that Dewey seems to hold that (b) is true. It is this manner of regarding (b) as true which is one of two ways in which (b) (or, indeed, any statement) can be held to be true, that I am calling (b_1). the other way in which (b) might be maintained to be true is not on the grounds that (b) follows from or is implied by a true statement. For (b) might be held as true on independent grounds; that is, facts or evidence of some kind might be supposed to warrant (b) as true in the sense that any statement of fact is held to be true or false. And it is this other manner of holding that (b) is true that I am calling (b$_2$).

Now although in general a statement, if it can be called true or false at all, is either true or false in the two respects just mentioned (and often distinguished as *formally* and *materially* true or false), it requires very little reflection to see that (b) cannot be true in the sense (b$_2$). And it is most unlikely that Dewey or anyone else should maintain (b$_2$). For in the particular case under discussion (b$_2$) would mean: "propositions are marked by properties of fitness and efficacy (and the opposite) rather than by the properties of truth-falsity" is true, in the light of such and such facts. And to substantiate (b$_2$) some facts should have to be introduced and exhibited. But wander as we may over the surface of the earth we shall never find any facts which may serve to warrant (b$_2$). The reason for this is that when we talk about propositions and how they are to be marked or defined, we are talking about how we propose the word "proposition" shall be used. Proposals to use words in certain ways, and by certain rules, are not subject to truth or falsehood in the sense that statements about facts are subject to truth or falsehood. It follows, then, that if (b) is held to be true or false it must be held for other reasons than that which we have called (b$_2$). And if the only other reason for holding that (b) is true is for the reason (b$_1$), then clearly if (b$_1$) is true or false, (b) will be true or will be false.

When (b) is held to be true for the reason, or on the grounds (b$_1$), it was said, this means that (b) is held to be true on the grounds that (b) follows from or is implied by (a). And (a), we are supposing, is true. For from the fact that tools are means and propositions are means it does not follow that it is necessarily the case that because tools do not possess the properties of truth-falsity, propositions therefore must also not possess the properties of truth-falsity. The reasons I gave for supposing that (b) does not necessarily follow from (a), to repeat briefly, is that although hammers, looms, chemical processes, etc., and propositions, may be regarded as *means* (and hence possessing the characteristics common to means), there is also at least one important difference between propositions and hammers, looms, etc. This one difference, I suggested, concerned the fact that propositions were formulations or symbolizations about material or procedural matters in inquiry.

From what has just been said it follows that (b) does not follow from, or is not implied by, (a). Hence (b_1) is false. And I have contended that (b_2) is also false. Therefore we may say that if Dewey's statement in paragraph P (or similar statements in Logic) means that propositions are not true or false *because* they are means or instrumental, or intermediary features of inquiries, by an analysis of at least two reasons for supposing these statements true, it does *not* follow that because propositions are means, etc., they do not possess the properties of truth-falsity. I am not, it should be noted, asserting that that part of Dewey's view which I have been calling (b) is in all cases false. What I have said is that if (b) (i.e., propositions are marked by properties of fitness and efficacy—and the opposite—rather than by the properties of truth-falsity) be regarded as true only on the ground either that (b) follows necessarily from (a) or that (b) is factually true, then (b) is false. Though there may be other reasons for supposing (b) to be true which I have failed, hitherto, to mention. These other reasons for regarding (b) as plausible or true, must, it would seem, depend on a somewhat different meaning or interpretation of those passages including (a) and (b) in paragraph P, than that which I have been giving to them. There is one other meaning to certain of the statements in paragraph P which is certainly worth mentioning if we are to do justice to this statement of Dewey's.

Although it may be true that (b₁) and (b₂) are false, it may be argued that (b) is true for the following reason: Propositions are either fit and efficient or the opposite and do not possess the properties of truth-falsity, *by definition.* That is, (b) may be either a direct consequence, or formulation of a rule, which has been proposed for the interpretation of what the word "proposition" shall mean according to some established usage. It might be asserted that (b) is "true" in just the same sense in which it is "true" to say "there is no greater number than 10" because we define "the greatest number" to mean $9+1$. It is hardly to be imagined that Dewey should wish to be understood as holding that propositions do not possess the properties of truth-falsity by reason of a definition of "proposition" or as a consequence of some definition. Definitions, it is interesting to observe, have just those properties which Dewey wishes to persuade us are possessed by propositions. Definitions are fit and efficient (or the opposite) and they are not true or false. Hence, if propositions are held to be neither true nor false by definition, that definition needs explicit formulation as well as the reasons for supposing it to be more fit and efficient than those definitions of "proposition" which allow every proposition to be understood to be either true or false. It seems, however, that none of Dewey's statements concerning the nature of propositions are intended as definitions. Indeed, so far is Dewey's discussion from proposing any explicit definition of propositions, that it might be said to be highly desirable if Dewey would formulate a definition of his meaning of "proposition." But it may be observed that so concerned is Dewey to draw attention to the instrumental character of propositions, that if these statements of his were interpreted as definitions of what propositions are, it would often be difficult to distinguish, on the basis of these "definitions," a proposition from "hammers, looms, chemical processes like dyeing" etc. And in his other statements Dewey is concerned to show that propositions are fit, efficient (and the opposite) and do *not* possess the properties of truth-falsity. If such statements were interpreted to be definitions, it would very probably take longer than one man's life-span to complete the statement of the definition. For taken as definitions, just the opposite course desirable in defining something is being pursued: i.e., defining propositions by stating the properties that propositions do *not* possess. For these reasons, Dewey could hardly be accused of maintaining (b) on such grounds and it seems unlikely that anyone else should wish to hold (b) to be "true" by definition.

I conclude for the moment, then, with these observations concerning the view that propositions, like hammers, looms, etc., "are marked by the properties of fitness and efficacy (and the opposite) rather than the properties of truth-falsity. . ." Each of the reasons I have been able to discover for holding this position (as stated in paragraph P) or for which it *might* be held to be true, have been shown to be false, except for the implausible supposition that the position is true by definition, which in turn has its own serious difficulties. Therefore, if this view concerning propositions which we have been discussing at length is true, it is very difficult to find reasons for supposing it to be true.

In view of what has been said so far, two important points deserve attention. We have already seen that the distinction between propositions as *formulations* and that which is formulated *by* propositions must be kept in mind. This might be made clear by citing an illustration. Suppose one is lost in some woods. Inquiry is concerned with devising or indicating a way out of the woods. In the act of inquiring as to how to get out of the woods one proposition might be of the sort: "If I bear West I'll be heading uphill." The proposition as such does not conclude inquiry, nor is its formulation itself the overt act of heading West. The act of heading West or heading uphill is also certainly not true or false. The proposition may be an efficient or inefficient proposal (and way of acting, were it acted on) for the end of inquiry. The proposition may be an important, or unimportant, *means* for that inquiry. To all this one may agree, as we have had occasion to notice before. But one fact has not, perhaps, been sufficiently stressed here. In addition to those features already mentioned, it should also be mentioned that it is the case that the affirmation, or assertion, or formulation "If I bear West I'll be heading uphill" is either the case or not. The *formulation* says "If I bear West I'll be heading uphill," and it is either the case or not that if I bear West, I will, in fact, also be heading uphill. The formulation says that the act of heading West will be accompanied by a certain feature (viz., uphillness) and the actual act of heading West will or will not posses this feature which the proposition or formulation says it will have. Hence, though the proposition is a meaning or an instrument in the inquiry it also has this feature; or at least there is every reason to think it wil have this feature. The view of Dewey, that the formulation will not have this feature, I have tried to show, by no means demonstrates or gives good reason to think that it will not possess this feature. For, put roughly, this feature of the formulation says that a certain state of affairs has a certain characteristic. When a state of affairs is said (or formulated) to possess certain characteristics that formulation must be either true or false. The formulation must be either true or false in this sense of the words "true or false": the state of affairs will or will not possess the characteristic which the formulation says that state of affairs does possess. Therefore: (1) *means* in inquiries are not true or false if what is meant by "means" is that which is formulated by formulations or propositions (in this case the act of going West and uphill); (2) propositions as formulations (as distinguished from what is formulated or being talked about) are either true or false in the sense just given. It is these two points which, though they have already been touched on previously, needed perhaps this additional clarification and emphasis. Point (2) is of course the point to which the entire preceeding discussion has been directed. And that discussion has been in the attempt to show that although Dewey regards (2) to be false (or misleading, mistaken, etc.) his reasons for holding (2) to be false are not convincing.

I now turn to certain difficulties that seem to be present in Dewey's view that propositions are not true or false, but the final stage of inquiry does have the characteristic of being true or false.

The above statement needs clarification. By way of clarifying it we are led directly to the issues I want now to consider. I have quoted certain of those statements of

Dewey's which are intended as formulations of the view that the properties of truth-falsity, if they can be applied at all, must be applied to the final step, or outcome, of inquiry, and not to the intermediate stage of propositional formulation. To quote him again, he says: "Were it not that knowledge is related to inquiry as a product to the operations by which it is produced, no distinction requiring special differentiating designations ((i.e., special terminology)) would exist. Material would merely be a matter of knowledge or of ignorance and error; that would be all that could be said. The content of any given proposition would have the values 'true' and 'false' as final and exclusive attributes. But if knowledge is related to inquiry as its warrantably assertable product, and if inquiry is progressive and temporal, then the material inquired into reveals distinctive properties which need to be designated by distinctive names. As *undergoing* inquiry the material has a different logical import from that which it has as the *outcome* of inquiry. In its first capacity and status, it will be called by the general name *subject-matter*. When it is necessary to refer to subject-matter in the context of either observation or ideation, the name *content* will be used, and particularly on account of its *representative* character, content of propositions." [44] I am concerned here with what is meant by saying "as *undergoing* inquiry, the material has a different logical import from that which it has as the outcome of inquiry." But a preliminary word must be said about an obvious difficulty in the above quotation.

Dewey says, or seems to say, that because knowledge is related as a warrantably assertable product of the operations of inquiry the *content* of any given proposition does not have the value "true" and "false" as final and exclusive attributes. It is, therefore, most perplexing when he goes on to say that that which he wishes to call the *subject-matter* of inquiry, is the material *undergoing* inquiry and not that which is the *outcome* of inquiry. In addition, he says: when subject-matter is being referred to "the name *content* will be used, and, particularly on account of its *representative* character, content of propositions." This is perplexing, because what Dewey *seems* to be saying is that the subject-matter of inquiry ("in the context of either observation or ideation") is, in its representative character the *content of propositions*. But if this is what Dewey means it would be the case that very few persons, if any at all, would ever hold "the content of any given proposition would have the values 'true' and 'false' as final and exclusive attributes." For—again distinguishing propositions as formulations from that which is formulated by propositions—the *content* of a proposition is that which the proposition is about; *the content* is that to which the formulation or the symbolization refers. To hold the *content* of a proposition to have the values "true" and "false" would be holding, for example, that tables, chairs, hammers, etc., as well as numbers, the sign for addition, etc., have the values of "true" and "false" as their attributes. It is clear that this is nonsense and that very few persons—even few philosophers—would maintain that the content or subject matter of propositions (in this sense of "content" and "subject-matter") have the values of truth or falsehood. But what would be maintained, as against Dewey's view, would be that the *formulations* asserting a content or subject-matter to possess certain charatceristics, have the values "true" or "false" as significant (though not necessarily "final and exclusive") attributes. If, therefore, Dewey means by *content of propositions* the subject matter undergoing inquiry, as subject-matter of either an observational or ideational sort, it is difficult to imagine anyone holding that the *contents* of propositions have the values "true" or "false" as their attributes. And it is difficult to see why Dewey attributes, as he seems to do, this view to anyone. It should be added that, in holding that formulations or symbolizations (i.e, propositions) are true or false in the sense previously explained, is not shown by Dewey to be necessarily denying that knowledge is the assertably warranted product of the operations of inquiry. Dewey may wish to claim this, he often seems to imply this to be the case, but this is a claim for which, as far as I have been able to discover, there are no conclusive grounds whatsoever.

Let us return now to the main issue facing us, and which is involved, I think, in what is meant by saying "as *undergoing* inquiry, the material has a different logical import from that which it has as the *outcome* of inquiry." [44] What Dewey seems to mean when he says that the material undergoing inquiry (the material, e.g., of propositions) has a different logical import from that of the outcome of inquiry is that truth and falsity are relevant to the latter but not the former. For as has already been indicated, Dewey holds that the settlement and close of inquiry is a state of affairs which may be designated, he says, by the words "knowledge" or "belief" but which he prefers to call "warranted assertability." Dewey also says "that attainment of knowledge, or truth, is the end of inquiry, according to the position here taken, is a truism." [45] In other places (e.g., in paragraph P) Dewey makes it clear that according to his view "truth and falsity are properties only of that subject-matter which is the *end, the close* of inquiry by means of which it is reached." Assuming that it is clear what Dewey means by holding that truth and falsity are properties only to the end, or close, of inquiry, we may consider some of the problems raised by this view.

The problems being referred to may be brought out in the following illustration. Suppose someone was interested in investigating the effects of changes in temperature upon various metals. He may begin organizing the materials for his inquiry (assuming his problem has been stated) by collecting rods of copper, brass, iron and steel. He then proceeds to construct an apparatus by which these materials can be subjected to heat and be observed (employing some means of measurement) to undergo changes, or to remain unchanged. Now in such an inquiry a number of important propositions may be formulated. There will be propositions of the sort "this is a bar of iron;" but I have in mind somewhat more significant propositions (based on this former sort) of the kind: "this is a bar of iron possessing such and such a length and such and such a weight." This proposition, it may be noted, is a means to determining if, when heated, there is any change in the weight or length of the bar of iron. The proposition is *not* the outcome of that determining process. As a proposition, it is either efficient or inefficient in aiding the investigation of a) whether iron exhibits any changes when subjected to heat; b) whether of copper, brass, iron and steel, all or some exhibit any changes when subjected to heat. Now it is also the case that propositions of the sort, "this bar of iron is now being subjected to so many degrees of heat" will be expressed each time the temperature is increased or decreased. In addition to these two propositions, an apparatus for measuring the possible changes of the material as it was subjected to changes in temperature was constructed, it was constructed on the basis of propositions of the sort: "either the bar will change or will not change;" "if it changes it will change in such and such a way;" "such and such a device will permit observations of such and such a change in the bar within such and such a limit." These propositions are only a few of those that will be entertained or formulated in inquiring whether or not, a bar of iron will exhibit changes when subjected to changes in temperature. And propositions of a similar sort will be formulated when bars of copper, brass and steel are being subjected to the same examination.

Some of the propositions involved in this inquiry will be, as Dewey says, about certain sensory materials, others will be about the ideational features of the inquiry. This difference being, presumably, that the former kind of proposition may be of the sort "this is an iron bar of such and such a weight," while the latter may be of the sort, "if the length of the bar is specified in terms of such and such a system of measurement, then any contraction or expansion of the bar may be read in terms of initial length $+$ or $-$ such and such a number of units of such and such a system of measurement." Now one may agree with Dewey that each and any of these propositions in this inquiry are means, instruments, or part of those operational agencies by which some conclusion can be reached. As such, these propositions have an intermediate function in the inquiry and none of them may appear in the conclusion when it is formulated. It is also the case that these propositions will either aid the inquiry in reaching some grounded conclusion, or mislead the inquiry and prove to be difficulties in the way to securing that end. But let us consider certain other features of these propositions. The proposition, "this is a bar of iron possessing such and such a length and such a weight," as an example, has at least one obvious but important characteristic. One thing we can know (if this can be rightly called a matter of "knowledge") about this formulation is that it is either the case that the bar possesses the specific properties of length and weight the formulation says it possesses, or it is not the case that the bar possesses these properties. And this, as we have already had occasion to notice, is another way of saying that what the formulation affirms to be the case, is in fact, either the case or not. I think we *can* and *do know* this much about any formulation which either affirms or denies some characteristic to be possessed by some state of affairs. Yet like most statements which seem so obviously and evidently true that they cannot seem seriously to be questioned, it is very difficult to *prove* this statement. Given some object O, one might affirm "O has the property p." It seems evident that either O does have the property p or does not have the property p. In other words, the statement "either O possesses p or does not possess p" seems clearly to be true. I say the statement *seems* to be true for some philosophers deny that it (or a similar statement) is true, though I find it very difficult to see how such a statement cannot be true.

This matter is important, for some philosophers who hold that some (if not all) propositions are neither true nor false, hold such a position on the grounds that in some (if not all) cases, statements of affirmations of the sort "either O possesses p or does not possess p," are not always true. It is beside the point, it may be noted, whether O *does* possess p, and it may be very difficult in some cases to *know* if either "O possesses p" or "O does not possess p" is true. This issue is a complicated one and we may not enter into it here. It suffices to say that the argument reduces to whether or not it is correct to define propositions as having the characteristic of being either true or false, and certain problems connected with discerning the proper application and function of the principles of contradiction and excluded middle.

These problems and all of the ensuing difficulties they might raise can be avoided and need not detain us here. For Dewey makes it quite evident that he does *not* hold to the view that propositions do not possess the properties of truth-falsity, on the ground of some particular interpretation of the principle of excluded middle. Indeed when Dewey discusses the law of excluded middle he has already formulated his view that propositions are neither true nor false. Hence he says of this "law" and those of identity and contradiction, "On the ground of the position taken, it follows truistically that they express certain ultimate conditions to be satisfied, instead of being properties of propositions as such." [46] And "the position taken" is such that propositions have already been described as not possessing the properties of truth or falsehood. Finally, when Dewey says, as he often does,[47] ". . . means as such are neither true nor false. . ." or "means are either effective or ineffective" he is making use of the principle of excluded middle as expressing certain conditions to be satisfied by means. He does not put forth his view of the nature of the principle of excluded middle as providing in any way the basis for his theory that propositions are not true or false.

Dewey might agree that the formulation "this is a bar iron possessing such and such a length and such and such a weight" has the relation to a given bar of iron such that that specific length and weight the formulation says the bar possesses is either possessed or not by the bar of iron. Since this proposition or formulation is a crucial one in the inquiry mentioned, Dewey would not be unaware of the importance of knowing, for the sake of that inquiry, whether or not the formulation is efficient or inefficient (or in our language, true or false). The inquiry will depend on the formulation being correct, i.e., in what it says about these properties possessed by the bar to be the case. But, Dewey would say, to know that this proposition is correct, will itself require an inquiry. Suppose we agree; we investigate and determine this proposition to formulate correctly the properties of length and weight possessed by the bar. Now with the aid of this proposition (and others) we may subject the iron bar to heat in order to observe possible changes. But this proposition in the inquiry is now the conclusion of a previous inquiry. Hence, by definition in Dewey's theory, it is no longer a proposition but a warranted assertion. Yet, though it be a warranted assertion, the assertion is still a *means* (and an efficient means presumably) in this inquiry, since the assertion is a crucial and necessary instrument for arriving at some conclusion concerning the changeability of iron when subjected to heat. Warranted assertions are true assertions, since Dewey has told us that the forming of warranted assertions is the end of inquiry and "truth and falsity are properties only of that subject-matter which is the *end*, the close of inquiry. . ." Hence we have here an example of a true assertion, or true formulation, which functions as a *means* in inquiry. Since the assertion or formulation functions as a *means* it is a proposition; since it is true, it is a true proposition. This example, then, would seem to indicate that Dewey cannot afford to shear the properties of truth-falsity from what he understands propositions to be without involving himself in serious difficulties.

Supposing our above example for regarding some means (or propositions) as true (and hence some as false) is, for some reason not acceptable. One may continue to offer others. Let us return to the illustration of the inquiry we have seen so far what is involved in the case of in-determining whether copper, brass, iron and steel undergo changes when subjected to changing temperatures. We have seen so far what is involved in the case of inquiring about iron. Similar inquiries will have to be conducted concerning copper, brass and steel. Suppose we have, by means of these inquiries, found that iron and steel expand on being heated. These warranted assertions: "if iron is subjected to heat it will expand," and "if steel is subjected to heat it will expand" are both *means* to determining the conclusion of the above inquiry. Brass and copper remain to be investigated. Here again, however, we have warranted assertions employed as means in an inquiry. For the same reasons, then, as have just been given we can say we have formulations which are rightly regarded as true propositions. We might find that copper, brass, iron and steel each expands when the temperature surrounding them is increased.

The conclusion, and final assertion about the expansion of all of these metals as they are subjected to heat, involves a series of warranted assertions about copper and brass and iron and steel. Suppose now someone wants to find out whether or not all metals expand on being heated. A *means* to that end will be the warranted assertion "copper, brass, iron and steel expand on being heated." But in this case a warranted assertion is being employed as a means or instrument in the inquiry. It is, then, a proposition; since it is *warranted*, it is a true proposition. Hence, again, we have an example demanding recognition of propositions as possessing the properties of truth and falsity.

In general, to summarize the point, whenever one inquiry employs the conclusion or warranted assertion A of some previous inquiry as a means or instrument for arriving at a conclusion, this warranted assertion A has the functional role and all of the features which Dewey assigns to propositions. And there seems to be very little reason why A, in such cases, may not be regarded as a true proposition. If this be acceptable, however, it follows, as against Dewey, that truth and falsity are properties of propositions. Or at least, that this is one more reason why propositions are best regarded as having the properties of truth-falsity.

Assuming that the above is clear, I turn now to a rather different sort of reason for thinking that Dewey's position that propositions are neither true nor false, though the conclusion of inquiry can be regarded to possess the properties of truth-falsity, is itself a position subject to serious difficulties. I will begin by choosing another example. Supposing an inquiry has been going on and has arrived at the stage where a problem can be definitely and clearly stated. The problem in this case being: "which of the following chemical solutions a, b, c, d, e, and f when combined with one of the others will yield the most rapid crystal formation of the sort F?" Here is a problem for inquiry, and the statement of the problem indicates much previous inquiry. It is already assumed that each of the solutions when combined will yield F; the problem being which yields F in the least amount of time. Suppose it also is known that the only possible combinations of a, b, c, d, e and f, which will yield crystal formation of the sort F, are: a combined with b; or c combined with d; or e combined with f. Now by means of propositional formulation of the following sort, this inquiry prepares for the act of experimentation. Experiment may proceed on the basis of the issues drawn up and made ready for experiment by the proposition L: "either (1) or (2) or (3), or (1) and (2), or (2) and l 3), or (1) and (3)" Where (1), (2), and (3) are the propositions:

(1) If solution a is mixed with b, the most rapid crystal formation of the sort F will occur.

(2) If solution c is mixed with d, the most rapid crystal formation of the sort F will occur.

(3) If solution e is mixed with f, the most rapid crystal formation of the sort F will occur.

(Notice that the proposition I have called L is a proposition which prepares the experimental stage of inquiry with all of the possibilities, each one of which must be considered. L is a proposition, not about the material conditions of the inquiry, but about the procedural issues to be taken into account. As such, L is a "leading principle proposition" of the sort which has already been discussed some pages back. L says in effect—employing Dewey's terminology—that either (1) or (2) or (3) will be determined by experiment to be grounded assertions, or (1) and (2), (2) and (3) or (1) and (3) will be so grounded. And what is understood by saying (1) *and* (2), or (2) *and* (3), or (1) *and* (3), is that the time taken for the formation F in (1), *might* be the same as the time taken to produce F in (2). Similarly the time taken to produce F when (2) is acted upon—when solutions c and d are mixed—might be the same as when (3) is acted upon—when solutions e and f are mixed. Also the time taken in producing F may be the same for (1) and (3). Now L would also indicate that one other possibility remains, the production of F by the various means stated in (1), (2) and (3) may all take the same amount of time. In the case of this result, (1), (2) and (3) would need reformulation, since none of them would produce F in any shorter time than the others. And the initial problem of the inquiry: "which of the named solutions when combined, in the manner specified, will yield the most rapid result F?" would then be answered in the grounded assertion "none of the named solutions, combined in the manner specified, yields F in a shorter time than the others.")

Now it should be evident that (1), (2) and (3) are each propositions, they are instrumental, or formulated *means* for arriving at a grounded conclusion. Supposing experiments are performed and it is found that: (1) takes 3 minutes to form F; (2) takes 15 minutes to form F; and (3) takes twenty minutes to form F. This experimental finding warrants a final assertion. The results show that (1) can now be held or asserted as a warranted assertion. It also shows that (2), (3), the other possibilities formulated under L (i.e., that "solutions a and b may produce F in the same amount of time taken for e and f to produce F" etc.) are all unwarranted assertions, or better are not warranted by inquiry. Now let us consider (1). In inquiry (1) was a proposition. That is, (1) had all the features by which Dewey tells us we may distinguish propositions. After the experimental phase of inquiry we find we have a right to regard (1) as a warranted assertion. Notice that as a warranted assertion (1) is true; it is true because it corresponds to the problem stated as "a solution answers the requirements of a problem" (Dewey's notion of truth).[48] Or it is true because it is a warranted assertion, and for reasons already given,

Dewey holds warranted assertions to possess the property of truth. So we are safe in thinking that by Dewey's theory (1) is true. Yet before the experiments were conducted the same (1) was, by Dewey's theory, a proposition, and hence neither true nor false. But this is certainly an unsatisfactory state of affairs and leads to very odd consequences.

Logically it means that at one time a formulation does not possess the properties of truth-falsity, while at another time is possesses the property of truth. Epistomologically, it means that a formulation is neither true nor false until by investigation of that subject-matter which the formulation affirms to possess characteristics of a certain sort, the formulation is *known,* or can be asserted, as true, or asserted as false. For (1) as a proposition affirmed "if solution a is mixed with solution b, the most rapid crystal formation of the sort F will occur." And (1) as a warranted assertion asserts "if solution a is mixed with solution b, the most rapid crystal formation of the sort F will occur." This warranted assertion answers or concludes the inquiry initiated by the problem already stated. But it is difficult to see how (1) as a proposition cannot be held to possess the properties of truth-falsity, while (1) as a warranted assertion can be held to be true.

What has happened to (1) from the time it was a proposition to the time it becomes a warranted assertion that it can be regarded as not possessing a property at one time and later to possess the property of truth? Can the stage of experimentation be said to add the property of truth, in this case, to a formulation which previously was understood to be without that property? And how can an experiment in any clear sense be said to add or create the property of truth as a part of a formulation when it is the *same* formulation that, before experimentation, does not have that property? Put another way, it is difficult to understand in what sense the occurrence of an experiment can be held to change a statement (or give it the additional feature) from one possessing neither truth nor falsehood, to one possessing either truth or falsehood, when the statement itself remains the same and unchanged. The heart of the difficulty lies in the position which would have to hold in this example that the same statement at one time does not, and at another time does, possess a certain property. But the *same* statement cannot at one time be without a property it later possesses. Yet (1) is the same statement as a proposition and a warranted assertion. Hence the difficulty.

These, and similar difficulties, arise in Dewey's view. If one held propositions to be either true or false, no such difficulties as these would occur. We would then say that the above case is one of those frequent examples of inquiries where all we know at first about a proposition is that it is either true or false. Experiments are conducted. On their outcome we may then know certain propositions to be true and others to be false (rather than merely knowing them to be either true or false). In short, taking proposition (1) as an example, at first all we may know about (1) is its meaning and that "(1) is either true or false." Later we may have more significant knowledge to the effect "(1) is true." The above difficulty disappears; (1) as a proposition, and (1) as a warranted assertion remains the same, (i.e., either true or false). But as inquiry progresses our knowledge about (1) increases; whereas at first we know (1) to be true or false, we later discover, in addition to this, that (1) is true. The formulation (1) remains the same; it is our knowledge of (1) that changes.

Which is to say that though (1) was true all the time *we* did not know (1) to be true until after the experiments mentioned. But because *we* did not know that " '(1) is true' is true" until experiments were conducted to warrant this, it does not mean that (1) was neither true nor false until we could warrantably assert (1) to be true. And it does not mean that we should not suppose (1) to be either true or false because we don't happen to know whether (1) is in fact true, or (1) is in fact false. Sometimes Dewey's words seem to imply that because we cannot assert (1) to be warranted, or (1) to be unwarranted, that *it follows* we cannot assert (1) to be *either* warranted *or* unwarranted. Yet it should be evident that this does *not* at all *follow*. For supposing one formulates a statement of the following sort: "Either there are mountains on the other side of the moon or there are not." Here is a formulation which would hold (i.e., would be true) regardless of what the results of any investigation of the moon might yield (except the most implausible result that the moon had no other side). Suppose, now, we reformulate this statement into the following: "An inquiry or investigation of the other side of the moon will determine either the statement 'there are mountains on the other side of the moon' or the statement 'there are no mountains on the other side of the moon' to be warranted assertions." Why should this statement be evidently true? It is because it anticipates by formulation the two and only two (hence all) possible conclusions to which an inquiry can come concerning the existence of mountains on the other side of the moon. Assuming the words "other side," "moon," "mountains," etc. to be determined and have fixed meanings, it seems very unlikely that anyone, including Dewey, would deny that there either are, or are not, mountains on the other side of the moon. Similarly, it seems hard to see on what grounds Dewey or anyone else, could deny the statement "An inquiry or investigation of the surface of the other side of the moon will determine either the statement 'there are mountains on the other side of the moon' or the statement 'there are no mountains on the other side of the moon' to be a warranted assertion." It is difficult to find any reasonable grounds for denying this statement. But this statement is merely a long way of saying: "The affirmation or assertion or formulation 'there are mountains on the other side of the moon' is either true or false." Or, similarly, "the affirmation, etc., 'there are mountains on the other side of the moon' will be either a warranted or unwarranted (i.e., not warrantably assertable) assertion." Now Dewey would be perfectly right in maintaining that only by inquiry can we assert " 'there are mountains on the other side of the moon' is true," or " 'There are mountains on the other side of the moon' is false" to be true or warranted. But no inquiry is required to assert " 'there are mountains on the other side of the moon' is either true or false (or warranted or unwarranted") to be true.

There is one objection that Dewey and those who hold Dewey's position might make about this statement. And that is an objection based primarily on terminology or definitions. If Dewey wants to define "warranted assertions" as assertions which are made only on the basis, and as a conclusion of some inquiry, then the statement " 'there are mountains on the other side of the moon' is either true or false (or warranted or unwarranted)" cannot be "warranted" because it is not, it seems, a product of inquiry in Dewey's sense of inquiry. That is, no inquiry concerning the moon is necessary to establish it as true. But I am supposing such a statement to be nonetheless true, and it is hard to see how Dewey would deny its truth. But if Dewey holds it true (or even false) he would merely have to use "warranted" in a broader sense, or invent another word similar to "true" or "warranted" which he could apply to such statements (i.e., to statements sometimes called "true by virtue of their form," or formally true statements).

Beyond this objection I fail to see in what respect Dewey might have grounds for disagreeing with what has just been said.

Now I have tried to show (using (1) as an example) that some statements or formulations may take place in inquiries as propositions, and the same statements may appear later in that inquiry as warranted (or unwarranted) assertions. This poses a problem for Dewey's theory, since if propositions do not possess the properties of truth-falsity, it is somewhat of a mystery how the same formulation when inquiry closes, suddenly may be said to possess the properties of truth-falsity. I have indicated that the way out of this difficulty is to accept the view that propositions do possess at least the characteristic of being either true or false. Inquiry disclosing the important fact of whether propositions are true or whether they are false. And I have suggested that this view deserves serious considerations; not only because it saves us from the above (and other) difficulties, but in addition because it is difficult to see how this view is to be denied. It is difficult to see on what grounds this suggested view, when formulated in general terms, i.e., "of a given formulation referring to certain characteristics of a certain state of affairs, that state of affairs will or will not possess those characteristics which the formulation says it possesses" is to be denied.

I will summarize certain of the above discussion as follows. Assuming the principle of excluded middle, we can say that of any formulation S, about certain characteristics said by S to be possessed by some empirical matter (or state of affairs), it is the case that the characteristics formulated by S are either present or not present in that state of affairs. And this is what is meant by saying S is either true or false. S is true when the characteristics said by S to be present in some state of affairs, *are*, in fact, present in the state of affairs (otherwise S is false). Dewey wants to maintain that the properties of truth-falsity are only present in the end *or close* of inquiry—as properties of warranted assertions. But I have tried to show:

1) There may be cases where inquiries employ warranted assertions of previous inquiries as propositions, as *means*, or instruments (having all the features by which Dewey describes propositions) to conclusions. A proposition in one inquiry which is a warranted assertion of some other inquiry would, it must seem, in view of Dewey's holding that warranted assertions have properties of truth-falsity, necessitate the conclusion (as against Dewey) that at least some propositions possess the properties of truth-falsity. The issue here depends on whether a warranted assertion of one inquiry can be shown to function as a proposition in another. I have tried to give examples of such cases; since Dewey holds that the conclusion of one inquiry provides the material and starting point for others, the point here can, without difficulty, be enforced by any number of examples where one inquiry employs as some of its instruments the conclusions, or warranted assertions, of one or more prior inquiries.

2) There may be cases of inquiries where what is formulated as a proposition appears later in the inquiry, in

exactly the same form and meaning, as a warranted assertion. This point may be expressed as follows: as *propositions* one may have "This is A" or "If A then B," and inquiry by way of experimentation may lead us to say of these propositions "This *is* A" or " 'If A then B' is true (warranted, etc.)." The only difference being that whereas before experiment we knew the proposition, after experiment we knew the proposition to be true (or in other cases to be false). This difference does not make a proposition different from a warranted assertion except in the sense that *our knowledge* of the proposition (or what the proposition refers to) has increased through inquiry. Thus if some formulation S is at one time a proposition and later a warranted assertion and hence true or false, and the properties of truth-falsity are not created by us, or imposed on S by our knowledge that S is true, or S is false, S must have at least been true or false as a proposition. For if S is first only a proposition and later shown to be a warranted assertion, it is difficult to see where S otherwise obtained the property of truth or falsehood. For if Dewey maintained any other view he should have to explain the difficult problem of how we or our knowledge about S or inquiry involving S, could impose, give, or add to S the properties of truth-falsity. I have attempted to clarify this problem by drawing attention to the fact that though in order to assert truly that "S is true" or "S is false" requires inquiry, it does not follow that before inquiry "S is either true or false" is false or mistaken. Indeed, to be able to find that it *is* the case that "S is true" or "S is false" it must be the case that S at least as the property of being either true or false. We can say more generally that a *necessary* (not sufficient) *condition* for finding "S is true or warranted" or "S is false or unwarranted" to be true (or warranted) is that "S is either true or false" is true. Now before experiment S may be in many cases, if not all, a proposition, and after experiment a warranted assertion. But if warranted assertions are true (or false) it follows that a necessary condition or property of S as a proposition is that it is either true or false. I suggested that perhaps on implicit reason for Dewey's rejection of the requirement that propositions be either true or false, is that he overlooks the distinction and implications involved between making this requirement a necessary, rather than a sufficient, condition of propositions.

For the reasons 1) and 2), if the above discussion has been in the right, I am led to maintain that Dewey's view that only warranted assertions, and never propositions, possess the features of truth and falsehood cannot be accepted.

In concluding, one point of a very general sort is worth consideration, for it has bearing on the previous discussion as well as on Dewey's view concerning propositions. This general point is as follows. What do we do when we set about, by means of experimentation, to reach some conclusion to a problem? Dewey tells us in a very clear fashion what it is that we are doing; we are trying out a plan of action (an idea or hypothesis) in order to determine if that plan of action leads to consequences which are such that they solve and settle some initial problem. The hypothesis has been formed as a possible solution of that problem; experiment is the way that hypothesis will be tested, or determined to be, or not to be, the answer to the problem. Now when these hypotheses, or plans of action, are formulated or symbolized discursively they take the form of propositions in Dewey's theory. (Whether *all* propositions are symbolizations of plans of action, e.g., "This table is red" etc., need not concern us here. What I do wish to say is that a plan of action which is to be experimented on, i.e., acted out, as formulated, is a proposition.) Supposing we consider this matter. In conducting an experiment E, we are going to determine if some given overt operation or action H will yield or lead to conclusions which solve some given problem. In inquiries there may be more than one H, and of course, in each inquiry there may be one or more E's before a satisfactory conclusion is reached. Now for a number of important reasons we may wish to formulate or symbolize every H. Language and symbolization of some kind is a necessary condition for the occurrence of inquiries. H when formulated may be called a hypothesis or plan of action. The formulation of H is a proposition, for the moment, called P_1.

Now when an H is carried on within the controlling features or conditions of an E, E may be said to be the act of testing, or a means to confirming or disconfirming *not* H (as some people are wont to say) but, strictly speaking, P_1. H sets the condition for E, these conditions are not confirmed or disconfirmed by E, but what is formulated (or, more roughtly, said, or asserted, offirmed) about certain characteristics, behavior, properties, etc. of these conditions will be determined by E to be the case or not. Hence, suppose H be the set of operations involving heat being applied to iron and the subsequent behavior of iron. These conditions, iron, heat, changes in the iron when heated, or non-changes, are neither confirmable or disconfirmable. They simply *are*, as some philosophers would say, or they are "neutral," etc. But P_1 formulates H to the effect: "If iron is heated it will expand." Now H has set the conditions for E. Suppose E be performed, and E discloses the fact that the iron expanded as heat was applied. E then confirms P_1, in the sense that on the basis of E we have a right to say "If iron is heated it will expand." When we say, E confirms P_1, we mean that by means of E and operations H, we are able to observe the fact: heated iron expanding, and this fact may be said to be (following Russell's usage) "the verifier" of P_1. By virtue of this fact, we know P_1 to be true or false (or warranted or unwarranted). If a fact or occurrence of this sort is called the "verifier" of P_1, E may be called the act of the "act of verifying" P_1. When we say we have, on the basis of information given us by the act of E, *a right to say* "if iron is heated it will expand," we are saying " 'If iron is heated it will expand' is true or is a warranted assertion."

Now we come to the point in question. Any act of verifying requires a P_1 to be verified. Any P_1 which is verified is said to be true (warranted), or false (unwarranted). Any inquiry, then, must in part proceed in this order: 1) P_1; 2) E (or the act of verifying P_1); 3) the warranted assertion P_2 that "P_1 is true (or false)." But it is evident that 3) asserts or formulates not quite the same thing as 1), for one important feature must be observed: whereas P_1 is about certain empirical matters, P_2 is about a proposition, about P_1. P_2 asserts that P_1 is true.[49] This is the somewhat more explicit meaning to the frequent assertion that when we set about verifying a formulation P_1, after the act of verifying it has been performed, we may say that the formulation P_1 is true, or (in other cases) that it is false. P_2 is a warranted assertion; inquiry and experiment warrant it, but P_2, though so warranted, is not directly about empirical affairs, but about a certain proposition, namely the proposition which is the formulation of a certain H and a proposition which a certain E (an E in turn warranting

P_2) has been devised to test. Warranted assertions, then, strictly speaking, since they are assertions about some formulated plan of action proposed as a solution to a problem, are of the form P_2. Warranted assertions (or the concluding assertion, the assertable product of the act of verifying some formulated plan of action, the assertable conclusion and outcome of a completed inquiry, etc.) assert that a P_1 is true, or that a P_1 is false (whichever may be the case when P_1 is tested). For one reason or another in some inquiry, E may be such that no warranted assertion, or P_2, can be arrived at. But I am supposing for the discussion that E does achieve definite results, results warranting P_2. Assuming this much, P_2 will have one of two things to assert. P_2 either asserts "P_1 is true," or "P_1 is false."

Now it is worth noticing that warranted assertions, or any of those final, concluding assertions of empirical investigations, could never themselves be true if the members of the class of formulations of the sort P_1 were neither true nor false, or if P_1 as a formulation was regarded as not possessing the properties of truth-falsity. Indeed *every-warranted assertion, every P_2, would be false,* since every P_2 asserts either "P_1 is true," or "P_1 is false." If P_1 is neither true nor false, then every P_2 is clearly false. If, therefore, as I have tried to show, every warranted assertion is an assertion of the sort P_2, it is false, if every P_1 is neither true nor false. Hence we are free to choose one of two possibilities; we can maintain either that every warranted assertion of every inquiry is false, or we can maintain that propositions of the sort P_1 are either true or false. And this, for reasons obvious enough to need no rehearsal here, makes it most desirable to hold that propositions, at least of the sort P_1, do possess the properties of truth-falsity. Therefore we may say (unless we choose to say that every warranted assertion is false) that a necessary condition for arriving at warranted assertions that are themselves true, is that the propositions which warranted assertions assert to be true (or waranted) possess at least the property of being either true or false (and not both). Now remembering that propositions of the sort P_1 are formulations of some H (some given operation or action) which in turn sets the conditions for some E, by which we can verify a P_1, propositions of the sort P_1 may be called "verifiable" propositions. That is, they are propositions which, roughly speaking, say something about matters of fact of one kind or another; they purport to convey some information about some part of the world of empirical affairs. They are such that what they have to say about some part of the world is subject to an act of verification (i.e., E). By means of acts of verification we can determine whether certain propositions of the sort P_1 are true or whether they are false. (I am not overlooking the fact that some of these verifiable propositions may be such that we lack the means, ability, instruments, etc., for performing an E to determine them at present to be true, or to be false. But if a proposition is verifiable it must be such that some E can conceivably be performed as verifying it; an E must be possible, if not at present able to be actualized.)

If propositions of the sort P_1 are propositions which purport to convey information, or formulate matters of fact, and are propositions which are verifiable (what they tell us is always subject to an act of verification) it must be added that these propositions include all of the kinds of propositions in Dewey's classification. All, that is, except certain of those propositions of a purely procedural or ideational sort. Ignoring these latter, for the moment, let us consider the former. These include propositions of the sort: "This is sweet," "This is a table," "Iron is a metal," "If it rains the crops will prosper," (each of which constitute one kind of existential proposition in Dewey's classification) and, in short, the class of P_1 propositions include all propositions for which an act of verification is a relevant and required means for discovering and warranting them to be held as true or as false. The only propositions which are *not* of the sort P_1 are propositions which are true independent of any E, which are true by virtue of their form alone. These propositions have no verifier, and they have no reference to matters of fact such that their truth depends in any way upon matters of fact. Whether Dewey includes any of these among his propositions having a "procedural" subject-matter, is difficult to say and has been discussed somewhat earlier. But outside of such propositions as are described to be "true by virtue of their form" all other propositions are of the sort P_1, i.e., they are verifiable propositions. Since, for the reasons stated, every proposition of the sort P_1 is either true or false, it follows that every proposition, except those that are true by virtue of their form, is either true or false.

We come, at last, to the general point which I have attempted to formulate and arrive at on the basis of the reasons given. Namely, that *any proposition about matters of fact, in being subject to an act of verification* by which we may have reasons for knowing (or holding) them to be true, or to be false (i.e., asserting them to be warranted), *must, by the very nature of these propositions and the process by which they can be tested, possess the necessary characteristics of being either true or false.* Therefore, all empirical propositions (i.e., of the sort P_1) or propositions stating some matter of fact possess the properties of truth-falsity. On the basis of this point, as well as the other points in the discussion preceding it, it would seem that Dewey is mistaken in holding that propositions do not possess the properties of truth-falsity.

As a consequence of this entire discussion of Dewey's position concerning propositions, I conclude: first, that the reasons for holding the theory are at best inconclusive; second, that there are very serious difficulties in maintaining it; third, and finally, that there are good reasons for supposing it to be erroneous. It is also to be observed, however, that the admission of the property of truth or falsehood to propositions does not seem to seriously effect Dewey's general position concerning propositions except on this single issue. In holding propositions to be either true or false, one can, without any apparent inconsistency, also hold with Dewey those other features by which he distinguishes and describes propositions in general, and formulates their function in inquiry.

SECTION 3.
THE EXISTENTIAL TRANSFORMATIONS AND
    MODIFICATIONS WROUGHT BY INQUIRIES.
BEFORE turning directly to the problem to be dealt with in this section some general observations are in order. In deliminating and introducing the issue we shall be concerned with, I think, a few words must be said by way of sketching in the related background and setting of the problem. For we are touching peripherally, if not directly, on what is perhaps *the* fundamental philosophic idea lying at the heart of Dewey's theory of inquiry. Namely that "all controlled inquiry and all institution of grounded assertion . . . contains a *practical* factor." [50] An idea from which many of the otherwise separate features

of Dewey's theory are brought in and related as phases in a process—a process which "effects *existential* transformation and reconstruction of the material with which it deals; the result of the transformation, when it is grounded, being conversion of an indeterminate problematic situation into a determinate resolved one." [51] No single point receives more constant emphasis, appearing in every chapter of the *Logic*, than that "judgment may be identified as the settled outcome of inquiry" [52] and "judgment is transformation of an antecedent existentially indeterminate situation into a determinate one." [53] This view runs throughout the *Logic* and is expressly stated in any number of passages. This should not be surprising when we remember Dewey's general definition of inquiry was *"Inquiry is the controlled or directed transformation of an indeterminate situation into one that is so determinate in its constituent distinctions and relations as to convert the elements of the original situation into a unified whole."* [54]

From these statements it is evident that inquiries are not made for their own sake; they are means to ends. Being instigated by indeterminate situations they function as the means to the resolution or settlement of such situations. This is not to deny that inquiries, like most means, cannot be enjoyed for their own sake; just as food and drink can be enjoyed for reasons other than that they are taken to sustain life. But means are not understood if their ends escape us. An obsessive delight with means which forgets ends altogether, or cancels the ends for which means were either created or discovered to function, is not the exercise of reason. When means become converted exclusively into ends for their own sake, or solely as ends-in-themselves, the result is pathological and not—as it is sometimes

maintained—the height of detached and speculative wisdom.

A. THE PROBLEM

Inquiries are not only the means to reshaping the material of indeterminate situations and transforming those
situations into unified wholes, but, Dewey says, "the doctrine that the original indeterminate situation and the
eventual resolved one are precisely *initial and terminal
phases* of one and the same existential situation, is involved
in every chapter of my *Logic* in treating every problem
taken up." [55] Inquiry thus, Dewey says, rises within, takes
place and is addressed to, one and the same existential situation. Certain important features of this transformation
accomplished by inquiry must be kept in mind. "One fun-
damentally important phase of the transformation of the
situation which constitutes inquiry is central to the treatment of judgment and its functions. The transformation is
existential and hence temporal. The pre-cognitive unsettled situation can be settled only by modification of its
constituents. Experimental operations change existing conditions. Reasoning, as such, can provide means for effecting the change of conditions but by itself cannot effect
it. . . The temporal quality of inquiry means, then, something quite other than the process of inquiry takes time.
It means that the objective subject-matter of inquiry undergoes temporal modification." [56]

The problem with which I shall be occupied in what
follows concerns the view that "judgment . . . is a continuous process of resolving an indeterminate unsettled situation into a determinately unified one, through operations
which transforms subject-matter originally given." [57] I
want to examine the position that inquiry effects existen-

tial transformation, or that when inquiry takes place "the objective subject-matter of inquiry undergoes temporal modification." I am aware that the view expressed in these statements has often been called and associated with "Instrumentalism," "the instrumental nature of thought," "instrumental logic," or "judgments of practice," etc. But it is not those views with which I will be (directly) concerned. Though it may be that it is from these more general views, or theories, that the particular position to be dealt with is derived, or is philosophically related. And because there has been a tendency to confuse various aspects of these more or less related philosophic theories when they have been put forth, either to be refuted or to convince others, it is important to be sure what the issue is with which we shall be exclusively concerned.

I have introduced our problem by quoting certain general philosophic statements of Dewey's. These, as I said, serve to place the problem in its proper setting. My special concern being to avoid, if possible, giving an interpretation to the problem or the theory from which it rises, which is other than Dewey's own meaning as he has stated it. So much of the criticism of Dewey, particularly on the fundamental issue we are to turn to, has been claimed (rightly or wrongly) to result from a misinterpretation of the notions being criticized, that I have taken time and some pains to set the problem in the hope that at least I shall not be held guilty on this count. At the same time I realize that part of what I will have to say in disagreement is disagreement on a view which Dewey regards as so fundamental to his philosophic and logical theories, that perhaps nothing short of an exhaustive treatise can do justice to the problems involved.

Dewey writes of his view: "the position here taken is that

inquiry effects *existential* transformation and reconstruction of the material with which it deals; the result of the transformation, when it is grounded, being conversion of an indeterminate problematic situation into a determinate resolved one." [58] This, Dewey says, is in contrast with traditional theory. For "the latter holds that such modifications as may occur in even the best controlled inquiry are confined to states and processes of the knower—the one conducting the inquiry. They may, therefore, properly be called 'subjective,' mental or psychological, or by some similar name. They are without objective standing, and hence lack logical force and meaning." [58] Two points are involved in what Dewey is saying here. These are (a) whether or not inquiry does "effect existential transformation and reconstruction of the material with which it deals . . .'; (b) whether if one does not accept Dewey's view, for one reason or another, one has to resort to subjective phychological explanations of what occurs when inquiries go on. Of these two points, (a) is the most important. I will consider it first and shall discuss (b) only to some extent by way of concluding the discussion of (a).

Some pages back (Section 1. The Problematic Situation) the point was made that Dewey's definition or formulation of the nature of the indeterminate situation is unsatisfactory. I said, and tried to show, that Dewey's account of these situations is such that it lacks operationally determined meaning, or empirical significance: in short, that from Dewey's formulation of such situations one has no clear idea as to what an indeterminate situation is. Supposing, for the moment, that the discussion there has been substantially correct. It would then follow that when Dewey says that inquiry "effects *existential* transformation

. . . of an indeterminate problematic situation into a . . . resolved one," that this statement too, lacks operational meaning or empirical significance. For it is a statement employing the same notion of indeterminate situation which, we are supposing for the moment, has been shown to warrant the criticisms mentioned. Hence one could raise serious objections to this position of Dewey's on the ground of the objections already raised in connection with a necessary and significant feature of this position.

Logically one would be within his rights were he to rest his case against this latter position of Dewey's, on the ground that the position employs as a fundamental part, the same notion to which certain difficulties were already shown to cling, and against which certain objections had been urged. These same difficulties and objections could be restated as arguments against this latter position. I am not proposing to take this line of thought. It is mentioned only to draw attention to the fact that Dewey's position here, and the discussion of it, is directly related to the discussion and issues raised in Section one concerning the indeterminate situation.

That his view, Dewey says, "is not assumed *ad hoc* but represents what certainly occurs (or is *vera causa*) in at least *some* cases, will be shown by considering some forms of common sense inquiry which aim at determining what is to be done in some practical predicament."[59] He then offers the example of a person who is ill. Deliberation and inquiry convince the person that a doctor should be consulted. "A proposition to this effect is equivalent to the conclusion that the consequences of the visit are calculated to introduce the interacting factors which will yield a desired issue. . . Hence the proposition when executed actually introduces intervening conditions which interact with antecedent existing conditions to modify their course and thus influence the issue. The latter is different from what it would have been if inquiry and judgment had not intervened—even if recovery of health is not attained." [60] But is it? Supposing the person discovers he has a severe stomach ache. This is the problem or existential *issue* to be dealt with. The person decides to go to a physician. He goes and may be cured. This might be an example in Dewey's favor. But the man might not be cured; then the issue, or situation, it would seem, remains unsettled. That is, the stomach ache, as an existential issue is not "transformed" into a resolved or settled situation, since, in this case, going to a physician has proven useless in the settlement of the issue. If "settlement or resolution of the issue" here means elimination or reduction of stomach pains, other courses of action might be considered. Or it might be the case the person dies from the pain. Or, on the other hand, he might never rise from his bed, and may conclude inquiry with an assertion to the effect that he shouldn't have eaten so much plum pudding the night before.

In either of these two cases inquiry can hardly be said to have affected an "existential transformation and reconstruction of the materials with which it deals." Except, curiously enough, considering Dewey's statements above, in a rather "subjective" or psychological sense of transformation of a situation; namely, that the persons knowledge about his pain can be said to somehow "change" or "transform" that situation of pain.

In this example the state of pain may perfectly well be regarded as a troubled, disturbed, existential situation. But it is difficult to see how, in some cases, inquiry can be regarded as working some transformation of that situation.

To these particular examples Dewey might reply that if inquiry is successful, then it transforms the troubled situation. But there are often cases of the above sort where inquiries conclude with the warranted assertion that no action can be taken which will relieve the state, or troubled situation, of pain. It is difficult to see how such conclusion can be said to transform the initial disturbed situation— except in the "subjective" sense just mentioned.

There is another somewhat different sort of problem which arises in connection with this statement of Dewey's. He puts forth the view that *all* inquiry contains a practical factor on the ground of "what certainly occurs . . . in at least *some* cases." But of course Dewey might be quite right in holding that inquiry has this practical, transforming character in *some* cases and yet wrong in asserting that *all* inquiries are of this sort. The statement of *all* inquiries containing such and such a feature, could only be *known* to be true if every single inquiry, past and future could be examined in order to determine the truth of this assertion. It is also the case that if one example of an inquiry could be found that did not have a practical character (i.e., did not reshape antecedent material, or effect "existential transformation") this would be a sufficient reason for regarding Dewey's view that *all* inquiries have this feature, as erroneous.

For reasons which are too far from our present problem to be discussed here, it has been shown to be convenient to formulate general statements about classes of natural occurrences and events, in such a way that these statements are not subject to the above formal objection. Consequently, it is generally held that the formulation of these statements should take the form of asserting what is *probably* the case. Where some theory of probability will, presumably, make expilict the degree to which we have a right to suppose the statements to be warranted. That is, statements of the form "all x. . ." or even "Some x. . ," if they refer to matters of fact should be replaced by a statement of the sort "the probability that x . . . is P" (where the value of P is defined in some probability theory). In view of such considerations one would like to see Dewey's statement about *all* inquiries, changed to assert something of this sort: "It is probable that if a given inquiry is controlled, it will contain a practical factor . . . etc." Or the statement might read: "In view of the fact that so and so many inquiries contain a practical factor; an activity of doing and making which reshapes antecedent material . . . etc., most inquiries will contain this practical factor."

Such a reformulation of the statement of Dewey's view saves it from the formal difficulty just mentioned. The reformulation rests to be determined on empirical grounds. It is either the case or not that *most* inquiries have the character Dewey asserts them to have. The statement is not refuted if a case of an inquiry is presented which does not have this asserted characteristic. This difficulty as raised, then, can be satisfactorily met by a slight modification of the statements concerning the partical, transforming, existentially effective character of inquiries. This much must be borne in mind when, later and after considerable clarification of other issues facing us, we can turn to reformulating Dewey's general position as to the nature of inquiry. It might be correct to assert that some inquiries contain this *practical* transforming feature, and some do not. Depending always on precisely what Dewey means by the reshaping of "antecedent material," or affecting "existential transformation"etc. Once a precise meaning is given to these notions the empirical warrantability of the view which they help to state may be determined. But that this kind of a revision might not satisfy Dewey is indicated by his concern, time and again, to speak, of *all* inquiries and *every* grounded judgment as possessing this characteristic of effecting existential and material transformations. Which leads me to inquire, in what follows, as to whether Dewey may be asserting a non-empirical statement when he speaks of *all* inquiries containing this certain characteristic.

Dewey writes: "All controlled inquiry and all institution of grounded assertion necessarily contains . . . an activity of doing and making which reshapes antecedent existential material which sets the problem of inquiry." [61] It is important to take note of the word *"necessarily"* in this statement. To say that inquiry "necessarily contains" a certain feature can mean several different things.

(1) To say that inquiry "necessarily contains" such and such a feature, might be taken as an assertion of a case of logical necessity. So one might say the statement "Jones is older than Smith" *necessarily* implies or entails the statement, "Smith is younger than Jones." The proposition "If Jones is older than Smith, then Smith is younger than Jones" being *necessarily* true. It would follow that by this meaning Dewey would be holding that all inquiries are such that the "activity of doing and making which reshapes antecedent existential material . . . etc." is logically implied, or is a necessary consequent of the occurrence of an inquiry. But this interpretation of Dewey's statement would not do. Dewey regards inquiry as an empirical affair and the phases or stages of the empirical process of inquiry cannot be considered to be related by logical necessity. He would not want to impute cases of logical necessity to physical casuality or change. Dewey also takes pains to offer evi-

dence for his view. But this interpretation of "necessarily" would render the whole position independent of any considerations of evidence or factual warrantability. This interpretation, hence, may be dismissed as quite evidently not one which would be in accord with Dewey's intentions.

(2) Dewey might mean to say that inquiry "necessarily contains" the "activity" mentioned in the sense that this statement follows from or is a part of the *definition* of inquiry. For part of the general definition of inquiry is that *"Inquiry is the controlled or directed transformation of an indeterminate situation. . ."* [62] In this case to say inquiry *necessarily* contains such and such a feature would mean that according to the definition of what an inquiry is, it follows *necessarily* that anything which is an inquiry will possess the feature of "doing and making which reshapes antecedent existential material." Which is to say that it follows by the rules of logic from the definition of inquiry that all inquiries "necessarily contain" such and such a feature. This follows in just the same sense in which it is the case that if men are defined as rational animals it follows that if anything is a man it necessarily contains the property of rationality.

While such a position may have the virtue of being the closest thing to an "eternal truth" to be found in philosophy, since no evidence—in the usual sense—can be brought against it, it is not without its own shortcomings. We have already had occasion to notice, in connection with a somewhat different problem, that an empirically significant statement (or statement of a position) cannot be content to rely on the appeal that it is a definition, or a direct consequence of a definition, to provide it with the cerdentials of warrantability. I cannot, however, attempt to state here in any adequate fashion what the formal and empirical conditions might be which definitions must observe if they are to achieve a significant place in the operations of inquiries. But one general feature is worth mentioning in this connection. Definitions have an obvious value when they enable us to locate and describe in a relatively simple way, by means of certain common traits, the multitudes of particular things that engage us each day of our experiencing life, and which become matters for communication among men.

A definition of a term is going to have some value if it enables one, without considerable confusion, to know what function or role the term has in discursive contexts, or to know to what conditions the word may apply and what conditions will be excluded when the term is employed to designate something. Consider for the moment the class of words called "object words" or words designating certain physical events or occurrences. It may be of value, e.g., to employ the word "electricity" to designate physical occurrences of a certain specific kind that have come to the attention of experiencing human beings. The word may first be defined as applying to amber in connection primarily with certain characteristics exhibited when amber is subjected to friction. Later experience may demand that the term, to remain significant, be regarded to apply to a kind of fluid as the agent of certain specific forms of physical behavior. Finally, the term may gain an even more adequate definition as referring to a certain kind of physical behavior specified by Maxwell's equations. Definitions of a term may change for the practical reason of enabling more adequate communication about experienced affairs. We may want to define man as a rational animal, but the value of the definition will be questioned when doubt occurs as to whether the term "man" can be applied to something that has in every other respect the properties which accompany that designated by the word "man," except that the creature in question is not rational. If such cases of doubt concerning the application of a term occur frequently it may be convenient to fix or redefine the term in such a way that prolonged questions as to its applicability are eliminated. Precision of terms in discourse has a direct bearing upon the adequacy of communication and the effectiveness of inquiries.

These obvious remarks indicate one desirable feature to be possessed by a given definition. Namely that the term defined specify or designate certain features in human experience and allow, without confusion, communication about those features. Thus, again, the definition of man as a rational animal may be inadequate; for there are cases that arise where a creature possesses every feature associated with that designated by "man," except that of rationality. It is an arbitrary preservation of a definition at the expense of clarity in communication to then maintain that the creature is not a man because the word "man" has been defined in such a way as to necessitate the exclusion of such cases. The definition is saved, but discourse is consequently rendered that such more difficult in the aessignment of terms to things be experienced.

For these reasons, if Dewey defines inquiry in such a way that the definition necessarily involves or entails the notion of inquiry effecting an "existential transformation," I should say the definition is inadequate. For there seem to be cases where investigations occur, having all of the features described by Dewey as making up the pattern of inquiries, except one. That one feature is that the investigations do not effect an "existential transformation," or reshaping of the antecedent material which sets the problem of the investigation. If, assuming for the moment there are such cases, these investigations are excluded from what are called "inquiries" on the grounds that they do not quite meet the requirements of the definition of what it is to be an inquiry, no great benefit results to the study of how men go about employing a method of reflective behavior for the solution of problems. These considerations are not new and they would seem to be in accord with the empirical spirit of all of Dewey's writings on the subject of inquiry and how men think. The crucial issue, then, is whether examples can be given of cases where "inquiries" take place, but do not effect existential transformation.

(3) Before turning to consider the reasons I hope to adduce as indicating certain needed changes in this view of Dewey's as he has stated it, one other possible meaning of "necessarily" must be dealt with. We have just seen that there are two logically possible senses in which Dewey's statement that inquiries "necessarily contain" such and such a character, might be intended. The third and last interpretation of the meaning of the word might be called a "physical" sense of "necessarily." Accordingly, by this sense of the word, a statement about some matter of fact, or state of affairs, is "necessary" if it is warranted or in accordance with matters of fact. Such a statement might be called empirically necessary, and a denial of such statements involves, not a denial of the rules of logic, but a factually false statement or an empirical falsehood. Thus if it is empirically the case that two freely falling bodies of unequal masses, under specified conditions, will fall with an equal rate of speed, denial of this statement would be falsified by factual evidence. These "physically necessary" statements would, it is evident, be merely another name

for the class of all empirically true statements. It is well known that the reasons for supposing any statement to belong to this class depends on evidence of a factual sort for the statement. It is equally well known that one can never be *certain* (in any formal sense) that any given statement belongs to this class. And it is very difficult to know, in some circumstances, whether a statement belongs to this class. Hence when Dewey says that inquiries "necessarily contain" such and such a character the question as to whether inquiries *do* contain this character—by this meaning of "necessarily"—remains to be settled on empirical grounds. Here, as in the second possible interpretation of Dewey's statement the issue can be settled if cases can be cited, which can rightly be called occurrences of inquiries where no existential transformation of a situation is affected by the conclusion of inquiry.

I will proceed, then, with an attempt to offer an adequate illustration of inquiry which does not have this feature which Dewey says all inquiries necessarily contain. A word of clarification is in order, however. I shall purposely avoid saying that *judgments,* or judgments of practice, as the concluding phases of inquiry, do *not* in *some* cases result in existentially transforming the materials of inquiry. Again the reason for this is that Dewey *defines* judgment and judgments of practice as doing just that. Thus what I want to be understood as concerned with here is whether or not there may be cases of inquiries of a practical sort which conclude with a solution to a problem, but which cannot ordinarily be said to have exercised any existential transformation of the material with which it deals.

B. AN INQUIRY CONSIDERED

Let us first introduce an example of a practical inquiry and then considers what consequences may have a bearing on Dewey's view concerning the efficacious nature of inquiry.

I offered (in Chapter II, Section 2) an example of a child placed in a maze. The child and various conditions imposed by the maze make up, we said, the *situation*. The problem, or issue to be settled, is that of locating a way out of the maze. Once the child is aware of the problem he may begin inquiry. Certain factual materials and circumstances of the situation may give rise to suggestions. Various suggestions may be considered and some may indicate new facts, etc. In short, the pattern of inquiry as Dewey has formulated it, may take place. Suppose at some point a plan is reached which seems clearly more relevant and comprehensive than any of the other possible plans of action. This plan is enacted, or an act of judgment occurs. Suppose further this movement according to plan leads the child out of the maze. What has happened? Inquiry has produced the means by which the problem generating it has been solved or settled. Or better, a problematic situation started off inquiry, which in turn led to a plan of action, which, on being acted out solved, or settled, or concluded the problem.

Inquiry in this case has been successful; it led to overt activity of such a nature that a problematic situation was settled or closed. In all of this one can agree to what Dewey has said about the characteristic progress of inquiries. But what does it mean when Dewey further tells us that this inquiry—as an inquiry—has effected "*existential* transformation and reconstruction of the material with which it

deals; the result of the transformation, when it is grounded, being conversion of an indeterminate problematic situation into a determinate resolved one"? What does this,
or any of the other similar statements of this sort which have
been mentioned above, mean? It is to be noticed, for one
thing, that Dewey is not, apparently, saying the *transformation* he speaks of *is* just the fact of a problematic situation having become, in time, settled or converted into a
resolved one. For he says that it is a *result of* this transformation—a transformation already effected and grounded—
that conversion of an indeterminate into a determinate situation is accomplished. That is, first a problematic situation takes place, then inquiry transforms the material—"an
activity of doing and making which reshapes antecedent
material"—on the basis of this transformation the problematic is converted into a determinate resolved situation.
But it is hard to see how this view describes what actually
occurred in the above example of an inquiry, except in a
trivial sense.

a) It may be said that a "transformation and reconstruction of the material" with which inquiry dealt had occurred in one sense. The child in the maze may have, in
the course of his inquiry, marked the walls, left them with
scratched surfaces, he may have bruised his hands and
scuffled the dirt on the floors, etc. In this sense some of the
materials with which inquiry deals were "transformed."
Also, when the child has arrived outside of the maze his
relation to the maze (i.e., his *spatial* relation) has changed
from what it was when inquiry began. Some of the constituents of the problem situation have been "transformed"
or have different relations to each other than before inquiry began. One can cite many such changes that have
occurred in this existential situation. But surely these are

hardly "changes" which warrant the description of inquiry as "effecting existential transformation and reconstruction . . . etc." Some better reasons for describing and emphasizing the situation as transformed and reconstructed must be given than these. For these "changes" can occur without an inquiry whatsoever. They are not significant results of, or even dependent upon, the instigation of inquiries.

Another similar "change" is that since inquiries take time, the situation might be said to be "changed" or "transformed" in the sense that it could be said that the situation and materials of an inquiry at 10:00 in the morning are "different" from what these will be at 10:30 the same morning, since the respective times are different. (Here, however, Dewey has told us that the "temporal quality of inquiry means . . . something quite other than that the process of inquiry takes time. It means that the objective subject-matter of inquiry undergoes temporal modification." The problem of what it is that has been "modified" in the above example, however, remains somewhat of a mystery.) One can agree, if these are the sort of meanings to the statements that inquiries transform, or effect existential changes of their subject matters, that such seems to be the case. One can easily agree because the position is then reduced to asserting little more than a trivial and commonplace fact.

b) But certainly Dewey would not want to rest what he considers a very significant feature of inquiry on such desperately obvious and insignificant grounds as those just mentioned. For the whole position being entertained is then hardly worth formulating. What other sense could Dewey have in mind in putting forth this particular view? The material of inquiry could be said to be transformed and reconstructed in the sense that a situation for which a solution is sought and one in which a solution is found may be observed to constitute conditions with respect to which human behavior will be quite different. That is, if one of the constituents of a problematic situation is a human being he will behave differently in that situation (and with respct to the other constituents in the situation) if he has (or knows) a solution to the problem making up the situation, than if he doesn't have such a solution. But if this should be what Dewey means it is equally difficult to see how this difference in behavior can be regarded as an adequate reason for describing inquiry as effecting existential transformation and reconstruction of the materials with which it deals. The child in the maze, if he discovers a way out, can hardly be said to be effecting an existential transformation of the conditions imposed by the maze. The maze is still a maze, though *we* may have knowledge enabling us to adjust and behave in such a way that the maze does not create a problematic situation for us.

Can differences in human response and behavior be rightly said to constitute existential transformation and reconstruction of the *materials* of (in this case) the conditions imposed by the maze? Can the maze conditions be said to have been reshaped or modified? Would not the "transformation" or "reconstruction" rather be exhibited or located in human responses and human behavior in this case? The walls and twisting paths of the maze have not been transformed or reconstructed, certainly not in any physical sense, and they constitute the primary materials to be dealt with by inquiry. Human behavior is, it might be said, "transformed" when inquiry is completed in the sense that the conditions making up the maze no longer constitute a problem, and the behavior of a person accordingly is not troubled or confused with the occurrence of these conditions. If then "the material" of inquiry means nothing more than human behavior, then as inquiries are completed, as answers are found to problems, these materials could be said to be "changed," "transformed," "modified" etc. through inquiry. But to say the "material of inquiry" is nothing more than human behavior is seriously inadequate. Clearly any inquiry will have to deal with at least some of those conditions which make up a problem and it is not human behavior which is itself problematic but the situation and conditions in which that behavior finds itself. These other conditions effecting and possibly effected by behavior should have to be included as matters which any inquiry shall have to reckin with if a conclusion is to be arrived at. To say that the material of inquiry is human behavior is to start off on the path to subjectivism and Dewey can hardly be accused of wanting to do that.

It would also be misleading to regard an individual's behavior with respect to certain existential conditions as, at a certain point, (i.e., after successful inquiry) effecting an existential transformation or reconstruction of those materials and conditions. And it would be a mere truism to say that because human response and behavior is also existential and part of a situation that when these change, as change they must if the creature is to remain alive, the materials of a situation have been transformed, reshaped, modified, etc. Indeed, with the exception of the trivial sense of "changes" in these materials already mentioned (i.e., their being scratched or scraped, etc.) the materials or conditions of the maze remain unchanged or what they have been all along. I am not concerned at the moment with cases of inquiries where it might rightfully be said that such changes as Dewey speaks of, are effected. For example, if the child set the maze on fire the conditions and material of inquiry could unambiguously be said to have been transformed. But there are cases where such transformations do not occur and these are the cases occupying us for the present. In the example, the material of the situation, the maze and the conditions it sets are unchanged, but the child's behavior can, perhaps, be said to have been transformed in the sense just discussed. This again, however, does not seem to warrant the description of the "existential transformation and reconstruction of the material" with which inquiry deals, as having taken place in the transition from problematic to solved or settled situation.

c) There is a third sense which might be Dewey's meaning of the position in question. It might be put in brief in the following way. There are indeterminate and problematic situations. Those situations generate inquiries. Inquiries, if they are successful, produce or provide solutions to these problematic situations. A problematic situation is different than one which is resolved or settled; the latter being a transformation of the former. This transformation is effected by inquiry. But though this seems to be what Dewey says, it does not aid us with the example we have been considering. The child and the maze make up a problem situation. Inquiry occurs and the child at length finds his way through the maze. When the child has found his way out of the maze *that* situation is different from the problematic situation, and this difference, Dewey might say, is the transformed situation-as-conclusion of an initial situation-as-problem. This, I repeat, would seem to be very close to Dewey's position as he has stated it. It would also then be the case that when the child is half way out of the maze the initial problematic situation has become half transformed into a situation-as-concluded. This may be the meaning of Dewey's position but several problems remain.

First, it is not any the more clear here what it means to say situations change or are *transformed,* than that the antecedent material which sets the problem of inquiry is *reshaped.* In what sense are situations *transformed,* and in what sense is the material setting a problem *reshaped?* To be specific, how can the child and the maze (as constituents or phases "of an environing experienced world— a situation" [63]) rightly be said to be *transformed* by inquiry? How are the materials, e.g., the conditions making up the maze, said to be *reshaped* by inquiry? One fact is evident. As the child overtly seeks his way out of the maze his physical relation to the maze is constantly changing. But a change in spatial relations hardly warrants the description of a "transformation" of child and maze. Just as walking down the street, after deciding to do so, can hardly be reported as a case of a man transforming himself and the street.

Dewey defines a situation by saying: "In actual experience there is never any such isolated singular object or event; *an* object or event is always a special part, phase or aspect, of an environing experienced world—a situation." [63] The problems increase when it is asked: how does inquiry, itself an event or phase of some situation, transform a convert "an environing experienced world" which is indeterminate, into a determinate resolved "environing experienced world"? Especially difficult is the problem here when it is remembered that inquiry and human inquiriers are included as parts, phases or aspects within this environing experienced world. To say a situation is converted or changed is to imply at least that the constituents making up a situation are converted or changed. But it is hard to know what this means or how such changes are to be known to occur unless they can be judged relative to certain permanent or unchanging features acting as some system of reference by which such changes can be specified, measured or recognized. To say "an environing experienced world" changes is not significant unless some bounary conditions and reference system can be specified by which such changes can be observed to occur and can be described. To speak of situations changing in some way while we and presumably our instruments, observations and inquiries are all constituents in—and hence parts of the changing situation—is akin to asserting that the universe shrank one half its size and instant ago. Obviously this would not be an empirically signicant statement since any instruments or permanent features by which such a change could be recorded are themselves subject to that change. No act of verification could conceivably be carried out to warrant such an assertion.

Returning directly to the problem, it remains obscure what Dewey means by saying the material with which inquiry deals is *reshaped* and *transformed,* or that the situation is converted, changed, etc. It is equally obscure how all inquiries effect the existential transformation of these materials, or how "the result of the transformation, when grounded" converts a situation in the way Dewey says it does. In the example of the child in the maze it is difficult to see how the maze and the material of inquiry is transformed, and how the child and the maze (and whatever else makes up that environing experienced world—that situation) are converted or resolved. Of course, it must be said, the *problem* is solved or settled. But the problem for the child is "What is the best way out of this maze?" The fact that a situation gives rise to a problem does not, it would seem, mean in any understandable sense that be-cause a *problem* is resolved, settled, etc., that the *situation* is resolved, settled, etc. What can be said to be changed or transformed, perhaps, is the child's behavior in the maze once the solution, or way out, is indicated to him.

I mentioned a trivial sense in which the materials of inquiry might be said to be transformed. An equally trivial sense in which a situation might be said to be converted, or changed, or transformed is that when inquiry reaches the stage of overt action and movement, physical changes obviously go on. But the case of a constituent (like a child) moving in some relation to other constituents (like the maze) hardly can be said to transform the *material* and *situation* of the inquiry. Therefore it still remains an open question as to what the meaning is of saying that "All . . . inquiry . . . necessarily contains a *practical* factor; an activity of doing and making which reshapes antecedent existential material which sets the problem of inquiry."

C. FURTHER CONSIDERATIONS

Let us try once more to find a solution to the problem of, first, what Dewey means, and secondly whether what he means is warranted. He has said, "All controlled inquiry . . . necessarily contains a practical factor . . . etc." Somewhat later he offers what, he says, "is logically involved in every situation of deliberation and grounded decision in matters of practice. There is an existential situation such that (a) its constituents are changing so that in any case *something* different is going to happen in the future . . . (b) just *what* will exist in the future depends in part upon introduction of *othe*r existential conditions interacting with those already existing, while (c) *what* new conditions are brought to bear depends upon what activities are undertaken, (d) the latter matter being influenced by the intervention of inquiry in the way of observation, inference and reasoning."[64] I will consider these points in the order of their appearance.

First, point (a) need not detain us. It is a truism that *if* things are changing then they are different in *some* respect at one time from what they are at some other time. Point (b) is not entirely correct. That "*what* will exist in the future depends in part upon" *other* conditions interacting with those already existing, is true enough. It is also true, however, that just *what* will exist in the future will exist whether or not any other conditions are introduced. Since if no other existential conditions are introduced to interact with those already existing, it still remains a simple truth that "just *what* will exist in the future" will exist in the future. I will pass over (c) and (d) leaving them as they are.

Dewey then gives an example (already discussed) of a person being ill in order to exemplify these four conditions. The problem for deliberation is the "proper course to adopt in order to effect recovery." Hence: "(1) Bodily changes are already going on which in any case will have *some* existential issue." Here Dewey says there will be an *issue,* where by his logical description, i.e., (a) in the above, he should say "something *different* is going to happen," it may come to an issue or it may not. But this is not directly to the point. "(2) It is possible to introduce new conditions that will be factors in deciding the issue—the question for deliberation being whether they should be introduced, and if so, which ones and how." It *may* be possible to introduce these "new conditions" would be a more guarded way of putting it in view what Dewey says in point (b) above. "(3) Deliberation convinces the one who is ill that he should see a physician. The proposition to this effect is equivalent to the conclusion that the consequences of the visit are calculated to introduce th interacting factors which will yield a desired issue. (4) Hence, the proposition when executed actually introduces intervening conditions which interact with antecedent existing conditions to modify their course and thus influence the issue. The latter is different from what it would have been if inquiry and judgment had not intervened—even if recovery of health is not attained."[65]

But in what sense is the issue *different* "from what it would have been if inquiry and judgment had not intervened"? The question may appear trifling. But not when we remember that according to what Dewey tells us in both point (a) and in number (1) of his example, change is going on, so that it follows truistically that at any one time the situation and the issue (or its constituents) is going to be *different* at that time from what it will be at another time. Hence in this elementary and formal sense since "an existential situation is such that . . . its constituents are changing so that in any case *something* different is going to happen in the future" it follows that the situation is going to be *different* in the future whether inquiry even occurred or not. Since the *issue* is that "bodily changes are going on" and these will "in any case have *some* existential issue" it follows almost by definition that the *issue* will be *different* according to how the issue comes about. Which is nothing more than to say if x, y, and z are the changing constituents of a situation, since the constituents *are changing,* they or the situation which they make up is in *some* respect different in the future from what it was in the past. But clearly then, it is no significant piece of information to learn that because bodily changes "will have *some* existential issue," that issue will be different from what it would have been if inquiry and judgment had not intervened, since the statement really tells us nothing more than that x would have been different if its history had been different. For what one wishes to know is what specific sense of "difference" is meant when it is said that inquiry makes a *situation different* from what it would have been if inquiry had not occurred.

It is of little help to an adequate understanding of Dewey's view here to be informed that a "situation is such that its constituents are changing so that in any case *something* different is going to happen in the future." For we are not concerned with "something" and "any case" but with the case of the occurrence and intervention of inquiry.

Another difficulty, and perhaps a more serious one, is that these statements (each of the logical points (a), (b), (c) and (d) and most of the explanatory statements in Dewey's example of the ill person) *would hold equally well for an inquiry that had completely failed of its intended purpose.* Dewey is concerned with case of "controlled inquiry" and "grounded decision." But it is also the case that, were a wholly ungrounded and uncontrolled inquiry to occur, it would occur in a situation where *"something* different is going to happen"; that it will be "possible to introduce new conditions that will be factors in deciding the issue"; that when "intervening conditions" are introduced "which interact with antecedent existing conditions to modify their course" the issue is influenced; that "the latter is different from what it would have been if inquiry and judgment"—in this case bad judgment—"had not intervened." Thus much of what Dewey says here would be true if controlled inquiries occurred, or uncontrolled inquiries occurred, or if no inquiry occurred. Consequently we are left with little understanding of what these distinctive characteristics of grounded inquiries, which Dewey speaks about, are or what they mean.

In Dewey's example he is perfectly correct in pointing out that the problem to be solved by the aid of inquiry, is, for the person who is ill, what steps should be taken by which conditions of some kind or another can be introduced into this situation of illness and thereby relieve, solve, or settle it. Deliberation convinces the person he should see a physician. A proposition to this effect would be, it seems, a statement that: if a doctor is consulted the desired conditions will be introduced and the situation satisfactorily settled. Judgment occurs when this proposition is executed or acted upon. Suppose the proposition proves to be warranted; i.e., the doctor introduces conditions which solve, cure, or settle the situation of illness. The doctor has then initiated certain new and different conditions into the bio-chemical situation of illness. The problematic situation hence becomes resolved or settled. But on closer analysis the difficulties of concern to us throughout these pages will be seen to linger. For when the doctor introduces certain elements, the bio-chemical conditions constituting the situation (or part of the situation) of illness is a changed situation. A situation made up of a certain specific number and kind of constituents is not the same situation when other constituents of a different kind are introduced. Let us continue to suppose that the changed situation is one in which the features constituting that of "illness" are eliminated.

No one would wish to dispute the fact that, in this case, a bio-chemical change has occurred. The question is: in what sense can it be said that inquiry in this case "effects *existential* transformation and reconstruction of the material with which it deals; the result of the transformation, when it is grounded, being conversion of an indeterminate . . . situation into a determinate resolved one"? What are the materials being *transformed* and *reconstructed* in this inquiry? Presumably these are the organic conditions making up what is described as the "illness." In this inquiry, then, these materials are "transformed" and "reconstructed" in the sense that they are eliminated. In their place a different set of organic conditions have been introduced or stimulated.

Perhaps this replacement of one set of conditions by another can be regarded as a "transformation" of the materials of the situation. In this case it might be, as Dewey says, that "the objective subject-matter of inquiry undergoes temporal modification" or "the unsettled situation can be settled only by modification of its constituents," or that the constituents of the problematic situation are "transformed," "reconstructed," "reshaped," "converted," etc. into a determinate, settled situation. The same occurrence, however, might be described in a clear way by saying that a set of organic conditions constituting a state of "illness' were, by way of reasons arrived at through deliberation and judgment, replaced or changed by the introduction of a certain different set of conditions which (directly, or in time) constituted a situation in which the elimmination of conditions of illness was accomplished.

The difficulty in understanding precisely how Dewey wishes to use the terms "transformation" and "reconstruction", in the descriptions he gives us of the fundamental traits of inquiry, may be due to the fact that these terms appear in an unqualified manner in these statements. That is to say, although it may be valuable to indicate the fact that all (or some) inquiries possess the characteristic of effecting some kind of radical change, some "transformation" of their objective subject-matters, it remains considerably important to understand in what sense this fact constitutes a unique and hence significant characteristic of inquiries. This difficulty and the resulting problems I have been raising here, is not so much one of the choice of the words "transform," "reconstruct" etc., as it is how these words serve to render the nature of inquiry distinct and in what respect they adequately enunciate and communicate the essential characteristics of inquiries in general. In short, to say inquiries effect transformations, like saying they simply change things, may be both true and important. But the significance of saying this much will not be readily evident unless the changes wrought by inquiries are explicitly described as well as distinguished from changes that are constantly going on in the world without the aid or occurrence of inquiries.

When inquiry as a process of organic-environmental-interactional behavior is referred to as effecting changes of some sort, a causal character is being ascribed to this process. The only sense, it would seem, in which inquiries can be said to have this casual property is in saying that inquiries at some stage of their development or progression, may lead the organism engaged in the operation of inquiry to over action of some sort. These actions are initiated ("caused") by deliberation—i.e., the whole nature of inquiry up to the moment of direct action is such that direct action of a specific kind appears as the next consecutive stage or step to be taken. It is the next "warranted" phase of inquiry. This stage of direct action—or judgment as Dewey calls it—may consist of directly reshaping certain materials of the problematic situation. So a sculptor, after deliberation, may begin to mold or reshape his clay according to some plan or idea that deliberation has effected. Or action, judgment, may be indirect in the sense of actively introducing different materials into a problematic situation; as a person who is ill might, by going to a doctor or taking medicine himself, introduce conditions which have been calculated to, in turn, produce a certain kind of result.

This would seem to be what is meant by saying inquiry "effects," "transforms," "converts," "modifies," etc. the constituents of a problem, or the subject-matter with which it deals, etc. Namely that deliberation *leads* to overt activity of some sort. That overt activity or behavior is physical movement of some sort on the part of the organism (Dewey calls it "organic-environmental interactions") and physical movement is going to have consequences of some sort among some existing conditions coming into contact with that movement. This much may seem painfully obvious. It is to be noted, however, that not only does deliberation "cause" or "give rise" to this physical-organic movement, but deliberation *and* this stage of action, *and* the consequences of the action are *included* as phases *in* the process of inquiry. Hence it follows by the very way in which Dewey has formulated what an inquiry is, that inquiry will "effect" existential transformations of some sort.

If this much be correct it becomes the more crucial when examples of inquiries are cited—i.e., of deliberation giving rise in turn to direct, overt activity—where the phase of activity does *not*, in any of the above senses of the words, "transform," "convert," "modify," etc., the subject-matter or material with which it deals. The child in the maze, we have seen, is one such example. A man might be lost in a forest. He deliberates and finally comes to the decision to take a certain course of action. He walks in a certain direction. He may come out of the forest, or he may have to change his initial plan and try another one. But in any case it can hardly be said that inquiry—the deliberation and the act of walking in a certain direction—"reshapes," "transforms," "modifies," etc., the material with which it deals or the material which set the problem for inquiry. The woods are not "modified" or "transformed" except in one trivial sense already mentioned. That is, as the man moves past trees and through glades, his position changes within the problematic arena called "the forest." But if this can be regarded as an example of inquiry "modifying" its objective subject-matter, it would be hard to distinguish that sense of modification" from any motion whatsoever; since any organic movement would also be "modifying" the same subject-matter. If the man blazed a trail through the forest, he might be said to be "modifying" or "transforming" or "reshaping" the conditions imposed by the forest. But this sense of "modify," "transform," "reshape," should then have to be designated as the sense in which these terms are to be employed—as against cases of organic movement (or any other kind) which might be said to be "modifying," "reshaping" etc., the material of inquiry.

It is of the utmost importance, and this has been the difficulty all along in grasping the full significance of Dewey's view, to know by what operations—what specific conditions may be located to fall within the defined boundaries of these descriptive terms ("transform," "reconstruct," "reshape," "modify," etc.)—one can discover whether or not these terms designate, or meaningfully determine some aspect or property of some given, occurring, subject-matter. The question remains as to whether or not these terms can be determined in such a way that they have some meaning and import when the general characteristics of empirical inquiries are being formulated, or whether they must be left blank and unspecified to be filled in at will in the context of actual occurrences of particular inquiries. In this latter sense the terms have no meaning except in reference to some one particular context and individual inquiry. But even here it is desirable to know in what sense (say) an inquiry into the effects of water upon a certain kind of cloth "modies" or "transforms" the material it deals with, and how this effected "modification" and "transformation" of material differs from any chance meeting of these two elements; as on some unhappy occasion a sudden hiccup makes the dinner guest spill his drink over his shirt front, effecting a similar "modification" of material.

Dewey says "inquiry effects *existential* transformation and reconstruction of the material with which it deals; the result of this transformation, when it is grounded, being conversion of an indeterminate problematic situation into a determinate resolved one."[66] One is led to ask: in what distinctive sense is the "material" of inquiry "transformed" and "reconstructed" and situations "converted" and "resolved," through the occurrence of inquiry? It is difficult to find out precisely what is being asserted and whether what *seems* to be asserted is warranted. For Dewey says inquiries *do* have this characteristic, they *do* function in this way and bring about these results. And holding that inquiries do have these features, he says, stands in "sharp contrast with traditional theory" which makes inquiry and the "modifications" effected by inquiry a matter of mental states lacking objectivity "logical force and meaning." But the particular question being asked, in spite of the above efforts, remains at best only partially answered.

D. SUMMARY

The entire preceding discussion has been concerned with two questions:

1) What does it mean to say that "inquiry effects existential transformation and reconstruction of the material which it deals" and that "All controlled inquiry . . . necessarily contains a *practical* factor; an activity . . . which reshapes antecedent existential material which sets the problem of inquiry" etc.?

2) Assuming that a definite or distinctive meaning of this position can be arrived at, how warranted is it to hold that all inquiry necessarily has the characteristics stated in 1), above?

It is evident that the answer, or answers, given to question 2) will depend on the way, or ways, in which 1) is answered. I have attempted to give what answers may be considered relevant to 1), and have in turn suggested how these various answers would consequently determine what is asked in 2), as to their warrantability. Certain illustrations were offered of inquiries not possessing the characteristics which 1) asserts of all inquiries. These have bearing on the validity of what is stated in 1). I will, by way of summarizing what has been said thus far, proceed to answer 1) and 2) as follows. As far as I have been able to discover, the answer to 1) is, in brief:

In every inquiry deliberation precedes and initiates, or gives rise to (effects) a stage of overt organic behavior or response. The phase of overt behavior consists of interactions between organism and environing conditions such that physical changes of organism and environing conditions results. When the physical changes are such that a problem instigating deliberation is solved, the terms "transformation," "reconstruction," "reshape," "modify" etc., may be applied to the constituents making up what is said to be physically changed, i.e., those features of a situation exhibiting the behavior of physical change (i.e., the objective subject-matter undergoing modification).

The reasons for supposing 1), as stated, to be warranted is the second question. Answers to it might be arranged in the following order:

a) Inquiry is *defined* in such a way that *if* anything *is* an inquiry it will have the characteristics stated in 1).

b) Empirically all inquiries are observed to possess the properties stated in 1).

c) Situations are *always* changing, hence the materials and constituents of situations will be transformed, i.e., *different* from what they would have been had inquiry not occurred.

d) Included in every inquiry is a stage of overt behavior. Such behavior causes organic-physical interaction. Hence the features stated in 1) are observed to occur.

e) The materials making up a problematic situation, and those constituting a resolved, determinate one, have a different status and meaning in inquiry. This difference can only be explained as a change in materials as formulated in 1).

These would seem to be the reasons for supposing Dewey's view, as stated in 1), to be warranted. Of these reasons it is probable that Dewey would regard b) and d) to represent primarily his reasons for supposing 1) to be an important and correct empirical observation concerning the nature of human inquiries. I have tried to show, however, that: a) cannot be accepted as grounds for warranting 1) since definitions cannot provide "evidence" for what is intended to be on empirical assertion.

As for b), it is a matter to be determined statistically, but I have offered two examples of inquiries which do not possess the features stated in 1) in any significant sense. Of c) it is evident that 1) is true, but only in a trivial sense. Since inquiry or none, situations are *always* changing we are not being told very much when it is said that inquiries change situations and material. The reason given in d) is ambiguous; it is not news that organic behavior will affect in *some* way *some* parts or constituents of an environment. The question is whether this behavior initiated by inquiry can properly at *all* times be said to "transform," "reconstruct," "reshape" the antecedent material setting the problem. These terms in quotation marks await some significant operational specification, if the statements in which they appear are to be significant. When the terms are given some significant status, counter examples of inquiries (e.g., the child in the maze or the man lost in the forest) can be cited where the material setting the problem of inquiry does not undergo "transformation" etc., at the close of inquiry.

In c) the statement made is typical of the difficulties we have had to face in examining Dewey's position. For it is held that there *is* a difference between indeterminate and determinate situations, and hence in the constituents of the changed situation. But the question remains: what is the difference and how is it described and stated in a way having operationally distinctive empirical clarity and significance? Terms like "transform," "reconstruct," "modify," etc., are introduced as describing (or defining) this change. But these terms remain unspecified. Hence it is obscure as to what they are intended to be specifying and in what precise sense this "change" or "conversion" of the material of inquiry is meant. New terms have been added which, since they in turn lack definite specification, merely increase the difficulties. Hence the warrantability of 1) and of what is said in e), depend on fixed, determinate meanings to the terms in question. It is also somewhat ambiguous to say that a problematic situation differs from one which is "converted," "closed," "settled," etc., since, again, these latter terms do not refer to empirically discernible features of the world unless they too become defined in such a way that they clearly indicate specific observable properties or traits displayed by existent things (This latter problem has been discussed in Section 1. the Problematic Situation.)

What has been said so far, however, must be regarded as very largely a tentative handling of these issues. But if the points I have been dealing with are at all relevant to Dewey's position, and if the above discussion has been, though provisional, substantially correct, it would indicate that Dewey's view is not, as it stands, empirically warranted.

E. INQUIRY: A REFORMULATION

In the light of the foregoing remarks it may be well to conclude the discussion with some proposals as to how Dewey's position might be restated in a somewhat more precise fashion and in a way which can be substantiated by an appeal to facts unobscured by the interpretation being placed upon them.

It is suggested (in Section 1 The Problematic Situation) that indeterminate situations could be described in a way having empirical significance, briefly as follows. There are at least two constituents to any problematic situation. These are a human organism and a physical environment. It was said that terms should be employed to designate one or the other of the constituents, but that a term would be unclear if we did not know to which constituent and characteristic it applied. Thus some terms might be called *behavioral,* they have reference to bio-psychological subject-matters. Other terms might be called *physical,* having reference to physical conditions and specified by physical operations of measurement etc. Now supposing this much to be clear one can proceed to reformulate Dewey's position in the following way.

First we want to state the thesis in such a way as to allow for cases which, I have tried to show, do not seem to possess this characteristic Dewey ascribes to *all* inquiries. Hence I shall substitute the word "many" for "all." The position would then be: many cases of situations occur where from a bio-psychological reference system certain behavioral conditions are present, defined in *behavioral* terms, such as "doubt," "trouble," "confusion," etc., which precede the behavioral activity called inquiry. From a physical frame of reference these situations exhibit properties which may be defined by *physical* terms, such as "unsettled," "open," "not hanging together," etc. These situations exhibiting *both* behavioral and physical characteristics of this sort are described by Dewey as "indeterminate situations." Such situations, moreover, often are observed to precede a certain kind of *behavioral* activity described by Dewey as "inquiry." That activity in turn is, in many cases, observed, from a *behavioral* reference system to bring about conditions defined in behavioral terms, such as "undoubtful," "untroubled," "unconfused," etc. From a *physical* reference system when these latter behavioral characteristics are found present, in the same situation the physical characteristics defined by such terms as "settled," "closed," "unified," etc. are also present. When a situation has these latter behavioral *and* physical characteristics it is a "determinate situation."

So much by the way of establishing what is meant by an "indeterminate" and "determinate" situation. One other preliminary matter must be dealt with before we can turn to the formulation of the thesis which concerns us. It must be recognized that inquiries are initiated and carried through to a close because of some concern or intent on the part of human being. Inquiries occur because human animals are able to make them occur. For it is certainly obvious that of all the constituents of any indeterminate situation, only those that are human beings ever move with intent from the disturbing occurrence of a problem to the anticipative responsive settling of it. Inquiry may begin and flourish in organic-environmental interactions as Dewey likes to stress. But it is not the concern of anything environmental (except if it be other humans) to carry on inquiry. Now to continue with the problem facing us. When a situation is "indeterminate" it has behavioral and physical characteristics defined by the respective terms, as stated above. Similarly, when a situation has certain other behavioral and physical characteristics (stated above) it is "determinate." Dewey says the indeterminate and determinate situations are initial and terminal phases of the same existential situation.

With these prefatory clarifications in mind the position may now be stated as follows:

When a situation has the behavioral and physical characteristics which define it as indeterminate, many cases occur where a behavioral concern (or intent) initiates a behavioral activity called inquiry, and that activity is such that it brings about conditions of a behavioral and physical sort which define a determinate situation.

This is a reformulation (and somewhat changed version) of Dewey's fundamental thesis as to the practical nature of inquiry. But some mention must be made of the words "brings about" in the above statement. Dewey uses the words "transforms," "reconstructs" material and "converts" the situation etc. In view of what has been said hitherto concerning these terms the matter might be put more clearly in another fashion. Organic activity (inquiry and organic concerns) as a behavioral occurrence may take a wide variety of forms depending on the particular problem and local circumstances of a particular inquiry. In some inquiries that organic activity may be manifested in a direct manipulation and changing of certain physical materials constituting the (partial) conditions of a problem. So a sculptor may directly manipulate the materials of clay, stone, etc. This organic activity, however, may also be an indirect manipulation or changing of materials (as when a sick man takes medicine which in turn affects the problem conditions making up his illness) to bring about a solution to the particular problematic situation. New materials may be introduced, etc.

On the other hand some problems may be such that organic behavior consists in adjusting in certain ways to the physical conditions making up a problem, without any activity constituting a physical manipulation or change of the occurring physical conditions, in order for a determinate situation to be reached. This would be the case, e.g., of the child in the maze. His behavior is observed to be made up of a flow of changing movements and adjustments to the conditions of the maze. His behavior is not such that it is directed to manipulate or change these conditions—in the same sense in which a sculptor manipulates his clay. The only "change" involved here is of a certain kind of behavior to bring about a determinate situation; in this case, to escape from the maze. It is probably also the case that any "direct" sense of *activity,* i.e., direct manipulation of existential materials is often at a minimum in certain of the sciences. In, say, astronomy or physical theory the activity of inquiry may be of a highly abstract character, on a very high level of organic response and behavior with respect to certain problematic issues. So mathematical inquiries may also be said to indicate activities or operations. But it is misleading to think of these as an *"existential* transformation and reconstruction of . . . material with with it deals" in the same sense in which a sculptor "transforms" his clay or a sick man actively introduces medicinal conditions into his system and "transforms" the conditions of his illness. Clearly the word "activity" here (when inquiry is said to be a behavioral activity) requiries much qualification and specification if it is to play a part in an over-all description of what occurs when an inquiry brings about a determinate situation. And of course if the statement I have given is to include cases of mathematical inquiries, the terms "indeterminate" and "determinate," as I have defined them, may need further clarification to cover cases of "non empirical" inquiries. These abstract inquiries, like all others, conclude (I should say) when the problems initiating them are satisfactorily answered. It is a questionable stretching of terms to say, as Dewey does, that a highly abstract inquiry into the mathematical expression of the physical notion of energy, "is a mode of *practice"*[67] (i.e., "an activity of doing and making which reshapes antecedent existential material . . . etc.")[68] simply because it involves "decisions as to what to do and what means to employ to do it."[69] Nor is that inquiry one of reshaping antecedent material because later its results aid the construction of atom bombs and the possible destruction of mankind.

To return to this reformulation of Dewey's view. Unlike the words "transform," "reconstruct," "reshape," "convert," etc., which Dewey employs to cover a varieay of contexts and inquiries, I would define changes of material, of subject matters and of situations, in terms of specified changes of either physical characteristics, or behavioral activity, or both in describing how determinate situations are brought about. But whether an inquiry, as a behavioral activity, be concerned to work changes of *physical* constituents (either direct or indirect changes) or to develop an adequate course of *responses* to physical conditions—i.e., whether it is directed to result in *physical* or *behavioral* changes, or both, in providing the solution to a problem—when the particular demands of a problem are met a determinate situation results. Thus regardless of the particular kind of activity that may go on, when inquiry occurs and is successful, a change has occurred: an indeterminate situation has become determinate. And this is what is meant to be described, noted, and conveyed by the words "brings about" in the reformulation of inquiry in the above.

Inquiry, whatever its particular organic direction and character may be, as shaped by a given indeterminte situation and the organic concerns initiating it, is an activity which (when successful) in many cases *brings about* the conditions of a behavioral and physical sort which make up a determinate situation. Thus the words "brings about" in this restatement of Dewey's thesis, refer simply to the behavioral activity which has occurred when a solution or answer has been provided for a problem or question. The *way* in which a determinate situation, a solution, will be brought about, depends on the particular nature of problems and inquiries occurring in the world at large.

This, then, is one way in which Dewey's position might be reformulated in a manner yielding itself to empirical determination. Of course, the specific terms having behavioral designations, like "troubled," "confused," etc., as well as those like "untroubled," "unconfused," etc., along with the physical terms that have been used (e.g., "unsettled," "open," "settled," "closed," etc.) remain to be defined. They must be given fixed meanings of a sort that the descriptions in which they appear will not be ambiguous or rendered void of any content having reference to recognizable and definite traits and occurrences to be found located in the world.

In this reformulation of Dewey's view the terms "transformation," "reconstruction," "modify," etc., have been eliminated. Such terms, for the reasons given in much of the foregoing discussion, are best banished from this general statement of the position. It might be the case, however, that in a description of some particular inquiry, one or more of these terms might prove to be of some value. When defined and determined to refer to specific behavioral or physical properties terms like "transform," "reconstruct" etc., may be aids in describing what occurred in the case of some particular inquiry. In this respect they might retain some value when accounts are given of how men think.

One last point remains to be commented upon. In drawing a distinction between behavioral (or organic) and physical characteristics of situations, and holding the distinction to be of fundamental importance, one might be accused of bifurcation or creating a dualism. One have not intended to imply, however, that the distinction between organic or behavioral and physical characteristics of a situation should create a chasm between these respective sub-ject-matters or that they should be marked off as two "realms" or worlds making up one situation. I have been concerned to suggest a clarification in language and in the descriptions of certain kinds of situations in which inquiry occurs. If no distinction of this sort is made the general descriptions of what inquiries are and how and where they occur is bound to be confusing. Hence my concern here has been the attempt to render such descriptions (or one of them) clear and empirically significant.

This attempt consists of making distinctions and examining how discourse is going to be adequately conducted so that a significant descriptive formulation of a fundamental characteristic of inquiry can be reached. But distinctions are not dualisms nor does concern with the clarification of language necessitate ontological commitments. It may be that what I have been suggesting in these pages, as to the way in which the instrumental (and transformational) nature of inquiry may be formulated, is not acceptable to the position Dewey takes on this matter. There is at least one passage in the early pages of Dewey's *Logic*, however, which would seem to suggest just the distinctions and constructions of the sort I have been concerned to trace and put forth in the above pages.[70] Whether what has been said here involves one in an unpleasant metaphysics, or drives us to regard inquiry as subjective changes of "mental states of the inquirer" lacking "logical force and meaning" remains an issue to be settled on independent grounds and need not occupy us further.

CONCLUSION.

I WILL summarize the main results of what has been said in Sections 1, 2, and 3. If the discussion in these pages has been correct it would indicate that certain important changes are desirable in Dewey's account of the indeterminate situation, propositions, and the practical nature of inquiry. I have not let the matter rest at that, however, but have in addition suggested somewhat revised versions of Dewey's formulations of these issues. This inspection of Dewey's views with respect to these three matters, and the difficulties found to occur with them, seems to demand some such revision of expression and thought as I have tried to put forth in these sections. It hardly needs to be repeated that these three themes with which I have been occupied are constituents having major importance in Dewey's theory of inquiry. This attempt to reconstruct the way in which these themes might be articulated should be taken as proposals which, if warranted, are intended to render the general theory of inquiry and, explicitly, these three parts of the pattern of inquiry: a) empirically more significant or determinate; as well as, b) more in accord with generally accepted procedures and accomplishments in the field of contemporary logical-empirical analysis. Taking a) and b) as two objectives, I have tried to reach them as follows:

a) By suggesting in Section 1 a reformulation of the indeterminate situation and, by extending those preliminary distinctions, in Section 3 formulating what empirically seems to be the case when inquiries take place. This statement arrived at in Section 3 may be regarded as a definition of the general characteristics of a situation within which an inquiry begins and ends. I have attempted to give an explicit description of the traits which determine just these kinds of situations.

b) By what has been said in Section 2: first, concerning the need for clarification of Dewey's general theory of propositions; secondly, and particularly, that Dewey's rejection of the notion that truth and falsehood are properties of propositions is neither warranted nor necessary in maintaining his theory of inquiry.

Taking these two points in the order above, I will restate the results of the discussion in the foregoing sections, briefly, in this way. First an indeterminate situation was defined as one which possessed *behavioral* characteristics (specified by the behavioral terms "doubt," "troubled," etc.) *and physical* characteristics (specified by the physical terms "unsettled," "open," etc.). These characteristics, as specified constitute the conditions which satisfy the description "indeterminate situation." In Section 3) I defined a "determinate situation" as one in which the behavorial and physical characteristics, as specified by the behavioral terms (such as "undoubtful," "untroubled," etc.) and by physical terms (such as "settled," "closed," etc.) are obsrved to be present. Once these behavioral and physical terms are operationally defined, allowing procedures of observation and measurement, etc., the existence of the characteristics designated by these terms—and hence the existence of indeterminate and determinate situations —becomes a matter to be determined empirically. The question: is such and such a situation indeterminate or determinate? is a question to be answered by applying the familiar techniques of empirical procedure.

Having specified what indeterminate and determinate situations are (and I assume throughout that Dewey's meaning of "situation" is clear and acceptable) it was then possible, in Section 3, to state the practical nature of inquiry as follows:

I. When a situation occurs possessing characteristics satisfying the definition of an indeterminate situation, many cases occur where a behavioral concern (or organic intent) is exhibited (or observed) in an activity called inquiry, such that that activity brings about conditions of a sort satisfying the definition of a determinate situation.

This is the suggested reformulation of what happens when an indeterminate situation gives rise to inquiry. Lest there be some confusion about what this general statement accomplishes, or the reasoning which prompted it, I will try to clarify my intention here in a few words. The formulation put forth here and at the close of Section 3 may be regarded as an alternative definition—not of inquiry—but of the practical character of inquiry. I have suggested, not how *inquiry* may be defined, but how, as an alternative to Dewey's statements, the situations in which inquiries move and have an effect, may be adequately formulated.

Dewey says that "the conclusion or end of inquiry has to be formulated in discourse, i.e., as propositions." In Section 2 these "intermediate means" were considered. After attempting to clarify certain issues concerning the various kinds of propositions Dewey wishes to distinguish, I suggested certain changes and additional features to Dewey's general theory of propositions. Section 2, D, dealt with Dewey's thesis that propositions are neither true nor false. In addition, however, and by way of indicating the desirability of holding that propositions are either true, or false, the movement of inquiry from the point of view of propositional formulations was touched on. That is, just as inquiry may be described as an activity bringing about the conditions satisfying the definition of a determinate situation, so from a more formal outlook and with an emphasis on the discursive and intermediate character of the process of inquiry, the same process may be stated as the construction with respect to a problem of propositions as possible solutions, their subsequent testing, and the conclusion arrived at as a proposition which is warranted in virtue of the intermediate operations which have produced it.

Of course Dewey makes it quite evident that on his theory inquiry cannot be regarded to be about propositions (except in the relatively rare case where a proposition is the problem instigating an inquiry) nor can the whole movement or pattern of inquiry be said to consist of propositions and the formulation of them. For there are conditions which are part of th process of inquiry which both precede and occur after the discursive phase of inquiry. Dewey is opposed to a widespread tendency to think of logic or inquiry exclusively in terms of the manufacturing, ordering and manipulation of propositions and discursive techniques. Once having acknowledged this much, however, and recognizing that inquiry looked upon as the formulating and testing of propositions must not be blind to other distinctions and characteristics, the process of inquiry described from a formal point of view may not be without profit. This being the character of the discussion in Section 2, particularly part D., what has been said there may be regarded as the formal counterpart—with the emphasis on propositions—to the above empirical description (i.e., I) of what happens when inquiries are born. The main results of that discussion of the formal structure of inquiry being:

II. Once a problem has been stated various propositions

formulating possible solutions to the problem may be put forth. These propositions were called "verifiable propositions" and on them acts of verification (i.e., experimental tests) are conducted. On the basis of what is revealed through an act of verification a given proposition is determined true or false. What the proposition asserts to be the case about some factual matter is found to be the case (or not) and to correspond to the problem as a solution or answer. On the basis of an act of verification ("judgment" is Dewey's word) a statement may be made about the proposition verified. This statement about the proposition is a "warranted assertion." A warranted assertion is, then, a proposition about a proposition which has been verified. The act of verification warrants the assertion "such and such a proposition is true (or is false)."

As a result of the discussion in Section 2 it can be said that there are three fundamental discursive features to a completed inquiry. These are: 1) the statement of the problem; 2) a formulated possible solution to the problem—a verifiable proposition; 3) a warranted assertion, which is a pronouncement about the verifiable proposition to the effect that it is true or that it is false. It also follows that, according to Dewey's theory of truth (see Chapter II part 2), a verifiable proposition which is shown, through an act of verification, to correspond to the problem as "a *solution* answers the requirements set of a problem" is true.

In considering the three phases of inquiry as discussed in Sections 1, 2, and 3 and the main conclusions of this discussion as stated in I and II above, it may be evident that I have attempted, by way of the revisions indicated, to restate certain crucially important parts of Dewey's theory of inquiry. Both I and II describe from a factual and formal point of view respectively the fundamental characteristics of the process of inquiry. If the issues I have dealt with are of considerable importance it should be remembered at the same time that there remain many issues and features making up Dewey's theory which I have either had to ignore entirely or have only mentioned in passing.

*   *   *   *

At bottom, what has been aimed for in these pages is the improvement in clarity and factual force of these primary parts of Dewey's theory. To have made any progress in this direction is not entirely without value, considering the value of the theory within which these suggested reconstructions might find their place.

For the theory itself renders intelligence articulate; an admirable accomplishment and a contribution to natural knowledge to be prized, perhaps, in a method-conscious age, beyond any of the end objects that intelligence as an instrument lights upon and discloses to inquiring beings. This is not to say that knowing has not been prized before in philosophy, indeed it has. But the subjective course of modern philosophy has been taken at this very point. On the one side the fact of knowing is identified with mind and inflated until it becomes the only world that can be known. On the other side, knowing, as evidently important in accounting for the nature of things known is acknowledged as such only with half concealed embarrassment. There is a self-conscious air to doctrines which, having the fact of knowing thrust before them, feel the need to find premises justifying this, as a kind of rational apology for what has been believed in from the very beginning. A philosophy which can ask in deadly seriousness how knowledge is possible, or whether we can know at all, is ill at ease at large as well as at home. Not even the world it construes and persuades itself to be the "real" can protect it from the rude shocks engendered when the dialectical journey it takes leads it to run full force against the stubborn rocks of the most obvious and common facts of experience. Here the momentum of doctrine, if it is to continue unhampered, must put reason and the candid recognition of abrupt and irreconcilable facts aside, turning these latter into mysterious concretions, unknown and unattainable.

Dewey has formulated his theory on the basis of what is observed and displayed in those domains where a method of thinking has brought about significant results. In the sciences the procedures governing investigations are not justified by the construction of antecedent first principles, but by the kind of consequences that flow from the use of such instrumental techniques. Regardless, therefore, of the particular shortcomings we may find in this theory, the very feat of putting it forth is deserving of our praise.

NOTES

CHAPTER I

* One can find many passages in Dewey's writings where the fact of the precarious character of existence is shown to have important consequences for philosophy and the role of philosophy in human conduct. Here are two such passages: "... It is difficult for the goods of existence to furnish as convincing evidence of the uncertain character of nature as do evils. It is the latter we term accidents, not the former, even when their advantitious character is uncertain. What of it all, it may be asked? In the sense in which an assertion is true that uncontrolled distribution of good and evil is evidence of the precarious, uncertain nature of existence, it is a truism, and no problem is forwarded by its reiteration. But it is submitted that just this predicament of the inextricable mixture of stability and uncertainty gives rise to philosophy, and that it is reflected in all its recurrent problems and issues." "Existence as Precarious and Stable," *Experience and Nature*, Ch. II, p. 45.

"Man who lives in a world of hazards is compelled to seek for security. He has sought to attain it in two ways. One of them began with an attempt to propitiate the powers which environ him and determine his destiny. . . . The other course is to invent arts and by their means turn the powers of nature to account; man constructs a fortress out of the very conditions and forces which threaten him. He builds, shelters, weaves garments, makes flame his friend instead of his enemy, and grows into the complicated arts of associated living." "Escape from Peril," *The Quest for Certainty*, Ch. I, p. 3.

1. *Experience and Nature*, p. 97. "... Nature is an affair *of* affairs, wherein each one, no matter how linked up it may be with others, has its *own* quality."

2. "empirically . . . there is a history which is a succession of histories, and in which any event is at once both beginning of one course and close of another . . ." *Experience and Nature*, p. 100.

3. Joseph Rattner, *John Dewey's Philosophy*. Intro., p. 153. The interquotes contain a passage from Dewey's *Experience and Education*.

4. *Ibid., p. 152.*

5. *Art as Experience*, pp. 14-15.

6. *Experience and Nature*, p. 4a. (Italics in original)

7. *Art as Experience*, p. 35.

8. *Reconstruction in Philosophy*, p. 86.

9. *Ibid.*, p. 27.

10. Dewey writes for example: 'Experience' denotes the planted field, the sowed seeds, the reaped harvest, the changes of night and day, spring and autumn, wet and dry, heat and cold, that are observed, feared, longed for; it also denotes the one who plants and reaps, who works and rejoices, hopes, fears, plans, invokes majic or chemistry to aid him, who is down-cast or triumphant." *Experience and Nature*, p. 8.

11. *Experience and Nature*, p. 4.

12. *Ibid.*, p. 9.

13. *Ibid.*, p .2a.

14. *Ibid.*, p. 4a. (Italics mine) Dewey has frequently defended his notion of experience, and what is experienced, as the prerequisites for knowing anything against the charge that this view commits him to a denial of our ever being able to know anything about the non-human world or pre-human history. One representative and satisfactory answer to such charges (as made by Morris Cohen, Bertrand Russell and others) is as follows. "According to my view, the sole way in which a 'normal person' figures is that such a person investigates only in the actual presence of a problem... All that is necessary upon my view is that an astronomical or geological epoch be an actual constituent of some experienced problematic situation. I am not, logically speaking, obliged to indulge in any cosmological speculation about these epochs, because, on my theory, any proposition about them is of the nature of what A. F. Bently, in

well chosen terms, calls '*extrapolation*,' under certain conditions, be it understood, perfectly legitimate, but nevertheless an extrapolation." *Problems of Men*, pp. 350-351. For a more comprehensive answer to certain of these problems raised by Morris Cohen: "*Nature in Experience*," *Ibid.*, pp. 193-203.

15. For example Santayana, in a review of *Experience and Nature*, says of Dewey that "it is an axiom with him that nothing but the immediate is real." "Dewey's Naturalistic Metaphysics," *The Journal of Philosophy*, XXII, 25, p. 683. (Later re-published in *Obiter Scripta*.) How Santayana uncovered this "axiom", or where he finds it at work in Dewey's philosophy appears to be no less mysterious than what the meaning of this axiom might be even if it were the core of some philosophic system. Dewey has replied at length to Santayana's paper in an article called "Half Hearted Naturalism" *The Journal of Philosophy*, XXIV, pp. 57-64.

16. "Common Sense and Science: Their Respective Frames of Reference," *The Journal of Philosophy*, XLV, 8, p. 198.

17. "Interaction and Transaction," *The Journal of Philosophy*, XLII, 19, p. 514.

18. 'Conduct and Experience," *Psychologies of 1930*, pp. 411-412.

19. *Ibid.*, p. 412.

20. *Ibid.*, p. 412.

21. *Ibid.*, p. 413.

22. That stimulus and response are interrelated, "that stimulates-as-stimulus depends on the response, as much as the response-

as-response depends on the stimulus, and that these work not as
an arc and disjointed part of a
process" but as a circuit, was
worked out by Dewey in 1896.
See his "The Reflex Arc Concept
in Psychology," *The Psychological Review*, III, pp. 357-370. His
main point then being that just
as a response is necessary to constitute a stimulus, so "what pre-
ceeds the 'stimulus' is a whole
act, a sensorimotor coordination.
What is more to the point the
'stimulus' emerges out of this coordination; it is born from it as
its matrix; it represents as it
were an escape from it" (p. 361).

This apparatus of stimulus, mo-
tor action, and response, Dewey
stresses, does not work as a string
of separate jerking movements;
it is a coordinated whole, functioning in and mediating experience. "What we have is a circuit,
not an arc or broken segment of
a circle." (p. 363). A circuit
within which fall distinctions of
stimulus and response as functional phases of its own mediation or completion" (p. 370).
23. "Conduct and Experience," p.
411. (Italics mine)
24. *Ibid.*, p. 417.
25. *Ibid.*, p. 420.

CHAPTER II

1. Bertrand Russell, *Philosophy*,
p. 3.
2. *Ibid.*, p. 4.
3. Bertrand Russell, *An inquiry into Meaning and Truth*, p. 15.
4. Bertrand Russell, *The ABC of
Relativity*, p. 213.
5. Bertrand Russell, *Philosophy*,
p. 159.
6. "Common Sense and Science,"
The Journal of Philosophy,
XLV, 8, p. 199.
7. *Ibid.*, p. 200.
8. *Ibid.*, p. 198. (Dewey's italics)
9. *Ibid.*, p. 199.
10. *Ibid.*, p. 201.
11. *Ibid.*, p. 202.
12. *Ibid.*, p. 205.
13. *Ibid.*, pp. 205-206.
14. *Logic: the Theory of Inquiry*, p.
66. Dewey adds to the passage
quoted: "The separation and op-
position of scientific subject-matter to that of common sense,
when it is taken to be final, generates those controversial problems of epistomology and meta-

physics that still dog the course
of philosophy. When scientific
subject-matter is seen to bear
genetic and functional relation
to the subject-matter of common
sense, these problems disappear.
Scientific subject-matter is intermediate, not final and complete
in itself."
15. *Ibid.*, p. 79.
16. *Ibid.*, p. 104-105. (Dewey's Italics)
17. *How we think*, p. 106.
18. *Logic: The Theory of Inquiry*,
p. 66-67.
19. *Ibid.*, p. 105.
20. *Ibid.*, pp. 105-106.
21. *Ibid.*, p. 27.
22. *Ibid.*, p. 106.
23. *Ibid.*, p. 105.
24. *Ibid.*, p. 105.
25. *Ibid.*, p. 107.
26. *Ibid.*, p. 108.
27. *Ibid.*, p. 109.
28. *Ibid.*, p. 110.
29. "Critical Common-Sensism," *The
Philosophy of Peirce: Selected*

Writings. ed. Justus Buchler. p. 301. See also: "How to Make Our Ideas Clear," *op. cit.,* p. 23. Especially such passages as: "... the whole function of thought is to produce habits of action ... to develop its meaning we have, therefore, simply to determine what habits it produces, for what a thing means is simply what habits it involves ... What the habit is depends on *when* and *how* it causes us to act. As for the *when,* every stimulus to action is derived from perception; as for the *how,* every purpose of action is to produce some sensible result. Thus, we come down to what is tangible and conceivably practical, as the root of every real distinction of thought, no matter how subtle it may be; and there is no distinction of meaning so fine as to consist in anything but a possible difference of practice." (p. 30). Or: a rule for attaining "clearness of apprehension is as follows: Consider what effects, that might conceivably have practical bearings, we conceive the object of our conception to have. Then, our conception of these effects is the whole of our conception of the object." (p. 31) Cf. also: Justus Buchler, *Charles Peirce's Empiricism,* pp. 108-120.

30. *Logic: The Theory of Inquiry,* p. 110.
31. *Ibid.,* p. 111.
32. *Ibid.,* pp. 111-112.
33. *Ibid.,* p. 115.
34. *Ibid.,* p. 112.
35. Dewey writes, for example: "Too

often, for example, when truth has been thought of as satisfaction, it has been thought of as merely emotional satisfaction, a private comfort, a meeting of purely personal need. But the satisfaction in question means a satisfaction of the needs and conditions of the problem and of which the idea, the purpose and method of action, arises. It includes public and objective conditions. It is not to be manipulated by whim or personal idiosyncrasy. Again when truth is defined as utility, it is often thought to mean utility for some purely personal end, some profit upon which a particular individual has set his heart. So repulsive is a conception of truth which makes it a mere tool of private ambition and aggrandizement, that the wonder is that critics have attributed such a notion to sane men. As a matter of fact, truth as utility means service in making just that contribution to reorganization in experience that the idea or theory claims to be able to make." *Reconstruction in Philosophy,* p. 157.
36. *Logic: The Theory of Inquiry,* p. 120.
37. *Ibid.,* p. 220.
38. *Ibid.,* p. 121-122.
39. *Ibid.,* p. 120.
40. *Problems of Men,* p. 343.
41. *Reconstruction in Philosophy,* p. 156.
42. *Logic: The Theory of Inquiry,* p. 345.
43. Sidney Hook, *John Dewey an Intellectual Portrait,* p. 101.

CHAPTER III

* *Problems of Men,* p. 335.
** *Ibid.,* p. 345.
*** *Ibid.,* p. 340.
1. *Logic: The Theory of Inquiry,* p. 107.
2. *Ibid.,* p. 106.
3. *Ibid.,* p. 67. (Italics mine)
4. *Ibid.,* p. 105.
5. *Ibid.,* pp. 105-106.
6. *Problems of Men,* pp. 328-329. (Concerning the source of this quotation see note 9 below.)
7. *Ibid.,* p, 328.
8. *Logic: The Theory of Inquiry,* p. 107.
9. Dewey has written that: "I used the term 'doubtful' in connection with the pre-inquiry situation, and used it as if it were a synonym for the indeterminateness I attribute to that pre-inquiry situation." This, he says, was "a loose use of language" and a mistake, since doubting "is, obviously, correlative with inquiring." (All quotations here are from *Problems of Men,* p. 327. This is reprinted from a paper by Dewey in *The Journal of Philosophy* called: "Inquiry and Indeterminateness of Situations," XXXIX, 11. This article being a reply to one by D. S. Mackay: "What Does Mr. Dewey Mean by an 'indeterminate Situation'?," in the same journal vol. XXXIX. Mr. Mackay also finds some difficulties in Dewey's notion of an indeterminate situation, though the points he raises are not directly related to those which I have been concerned to deal with here). This correction of his own language, which Dewey makes, does not bear very seriously on the par-

ticular issue under discussion; namely, as to the way in which Dewey formulates and describes what an indeterminate situation is.
10. *Logic: The Theory of Inquiry,* p. 133.
11. *Ibid.,* p. 121.
12. *Ibid.,* pp. 283-284.
13. *Ibid.,* p. 284.
14. *Ibid.,* pp. 289-290.
15. *Ibid.,* p. 290.
16. *Ibid.,* p. 290.
17. *Ibid.,* p. 291.
18. *Ibid.,* p. 274.
19. *Ibid.,* p. 264.
20. *Ibid.,* p. 264.
21. *Ibid.,* p. 268.
22. *Ibid.,* pp. 294-295.
23. *Ibid.,* cf. p. 256.
24. *Ibid.,* p. 272.
25. *Ibid.,* p. 277. I am assuming throughout this discussion that it is possible to distinguish *analytic,* or necessarily true propositions, from factual or *synthetic* propositions. Some doubt has been raised among a number of logicians as to whether such a distinction can be adequately formulated and, indeed, whether it is even defensible on theoretical grounds. For an excellent discussion of some of the initial and underlying difficulties making up this problem see W. V. Quine's paper: "Notes on Existence and Necessity", *The Journal of Philosophy,* XL, 5, pp. 113-127. Also see A. Church's review of Quine's paper: *Journal of Symbolic Logic,* VIII, (1943). See also: R. Carnap, *Meaning and Necessity.* This whole problem, whatever its final outcome may be, does not bear directly

upon the issues I am concerned with here. For whether the distinction between analytic and synthetic propositions can be maintained or not, it is evident that Dewey's universal propositions cannot be regarded as analytic in character. Thus the question of just what these universal propositions are remains open and will not be settled by a decision as to the nature or meaning of analyticity. If it should come to pass that the usual manner of distinguishing analytic and sythetic propositions cannot be sufficiently defended, many of the incidental remarks and some of the language of my discussion in these pages would have to be revised or regarded as erroneous. But we should be no closer to learning what Dewey's universal propositions are, and it is just this which I am trying to explore in these pages. Consequently, by way of illustrating some of these difficulties and problems, as well as providing a means to making some progress in this direction, I will assume that propositions can be said to be either "analytic" or "synthetic" according to the ordinary, if rough meanings of these terms. For an interesting suggestion that, in accordance with Dewey's general condemnation of dualisms, the dualism (and here it is argued that the distinction is a dualism) of analytic and synthetic in logic must also be done away with, see: Morton White, "The Analytic and the Synthetic," in *John Dewey: Philosopher of Science and Freedom.* For the best exposition of

this whole problem see Quine's brilliant paper, "Two Dogmas of Empiricism," *The Philosophical Review,* LX, 1, (1951) .

26. *Ibid.,* p. 272. (italics mine)
27. *Ibid.,* p. 278.
28. *Ibid.,* p. 271.
29. *Ibid.,* pp. 271-272.
30. *Ibid.,* p. 272. (Italics mine)
31. *Ibid.,* p. 272.
32. *Ibid.,* p. 398.
33. *Ibid.,* pp. 397-398. (Italics mine)
34. "A Symposium of Reviews of John Dewey's Logic: The Theory of Inquiry," *The Journal of Philosophy,* XXXVI, 21, p. 579. In his contribution to this symposium (pp. 576-581) Ernest Nagel raises three main points. (1) That the difference between universal and generic propositions cannot be exhibited in their linguistic formulations, but only by their respective functions in the context of given inquiries. (2) Dewey's choice of propositions as illustrating one or the other of his propositional forms—universal or generic — (e.g., the Newtonian formula for gravitation) is hence confusing; since in other contexts these same propositions may function differently. Thus whether a proposition is universal or generic depends on the particular function it has in a particular inquiry. Thus no example of a proposition, unless its function in the context of a specific inquiry be added, will satisfactorily illustrate one or the other of these propositional forms. (3) Dewey's use of the word "necessary" in connection with his universal propositions raises questions as to what that word means. These propositions can-

not be identified with the analytic ones of contemporary theory. As I have ventured to pursue these points in part of my discussion of this subject, I wish to acknowledge that the credit for raising them must be given to Professor Nagel. Though, at the same time, he must not be thought to be in any way responsible for the way in which I have dealt with these points and the subsequent discussion of them in the present paper.

35. *Logic: The Theory of Inquiry,* p. 399.

36. *Ibid.,* p. 275.

37. "What is a Leading Principle?" *The Philosophy of Peirce: Selected Writings,* ed. Justus Buchler, p. 133. Dewey says that in general he follows the account given by Peirce concerning these "guiding" or "leading" principles (*Logic* p. 12). But Dewey "follows" Peirce here in interpreting and emphasizing certain logical principles (e.g., the principle of excluded middle, etc.) as *habits,* or formulations of habits, operating in the organic process of inference, in drawing conclusions. He emphasizes the biological basis of these principles. Later Dewey says "These guiding logical principles are not *premises* of inference or argument. They are conditions to be satisfied such that knowledge of them provides a principle of directing and testing." (p. 13) In this discussion I have been concerned to emphasize the logical, rather than the organic, or biological side of Peirce's suggestion. Hence I am primarily interested in that part of Peirce's statement describing a leading

principle as "a proposition of which the antecedent should describe all possible premises ... while the consequent should describe how the conclusion to which it would lead would be determinately related to those premises." These leading principles *order* the premises and conclusions of an inquiry; they are not, and here I agree with Dewey, themselves the premises of an inquiry. It might be well to state here, however, that my interpretation of these principles and their function in inquiry, may depart considerably, if not entirely, from the purpose and interpretation Pierce had in mind when he introduced the notion of a leading principle. The notion of a leading principle, as put forth here, may be foreign to the meaning of Peirce and Dewey when they discuss that notion in their writings. My purpose in introducing the particular notion set forth is that: a) it deserves consideration when the nature of inquiries is being investigated and described; b) it seems to be, I think, very close to what some of Dewey's universal propositions are. Therefore, what I have to say concerning these leading principles constitutes, not a theory, but at best a tentative proposal, or hypothesis, designed to indicate the grounds for supposing a) and b) to be very likely, or at least worthy of consideration.

38. *Logic: The Theory of Inquiry,* p. 278. Cf. also p. 264. The proof of universal propositions as stated by Dewey is: "(1) the formulation of the idea suggested in a hypothetical proposi-

tion, and (2) by the transformation of data into a unified situation through execution of the operations presented by the hypothetical as a rule of action" (p. 278). It is interesting to note that this *proof* would apply as a means to testing the *value* (not the truth) of a leading principle for any given inquiry. But the difficulty here is that it is not clear whether Dewey intends his "proof" as determining the *truth*, or as determining the *relevancy* of universal hypothetical propositions.

39. *Ibid.*, p. 120. (The italics are added by Dewey when he quotes this same passage in *Problems of Men*, p. 339.)
40. *Problems of Men* p. 339
41. *Ibid.*, p. 340.
42. *Logic: The Theory of Inquiry*, p. 287.
43. *Ibid.*, p. 283.
44. *Ibid.*, pp. 118-119. (Italics in the original)
45. *Ibid.*, pp. 7-8.
46. *Ibid.*, pp. 343-344.
47. *Ibid.*, p. 287.
48. *Problems of Men*, p. 343.
49. The suggested difference here between propositions of the sort p_1 and those of the sort p_2 is important. For, as far as I can see, that difference constitutes the only defference on the basis of which a warranted assertion (i.e., propositions of the sort p_2) can be said to be different from—or not the same—as propositions (or formulated plans of action, hypotheses) of the sort p_1 which are to be, or are being, or have been verified. The difference is that while p_1 propositions formulate some hypothesis or plan of action, p_2 proposi-

tions are meta-linguistic: their subject matter (or what they are about) is made up of p_1 propositions. Or put another way, warranted assertions are meta-linguistic statements asserting some propositions (of the sort p_1) to be true, or to be false.

50. *Logic: The Theory of Inquiry*, p. 160.
51. *Ibid.*, p. 159.
52. *Ibid.*, p. 120.
53. *Ibid.*, p. 220.
54. *Ibid.*, pp. 104-105.
55. *Problems of Men*, p. 324.
56. *Logic: The Theory of Inquiry*, p. 118.
57. *Ibid.*, p. 283.
58. *Ibid.*, p. 159.
59. *Ibid.*, p. 160.
60. *Ibid.*, p. 163.
61. *Ibid.*, p. 160.
62. *Ibid.*, pp. 104-105.
63. *Ibid.*, p. 67.
64. *Ibid.*, pp. 162-163.
65. For all quotations in this paragraph see *Ibid.*, p. 163.
66. *Ibid.*, p. 159.
67. *Ibid.*, p. 161.
68. *Ibid.*, p. 160.
69. *Ibid.*, p. 161.
70. *Ibid.*, p. 31. Here Dewey writes: "What exists in normal behavior-development is a ... circuit of which the earlier or 'open' phase is the tension of various elements of *organic* energy, while the final and 'closed' phase is the institution of integrated interaction of *organism* and *environment*. This integration is represented upon the *organic* side by the equilibration of organic energies and, upon the *environmental* side by the existence of satisfying conditions."
(Italics mine)

BIBLIOGRAPHY

1.
WORKS CITED AND QUOTED

Buchler, Justus. *Charles Peirce's Empiricism.* N.Y., Harcourt Brace & Co., 1939.

——, ——. ed. *The Philosophy of Peirce: Selected Writings.* N.Y., Harcourt Brace & Co., 1940.

Dewey, John. "The Reflex Arc Concept in Psychology." *Psychological Review* III:357-370, July 1896.

——, ——. *Reconstruction in Philosophy.* N.Y., Henry Holt & Co., 1920.

——, ——. *Experience and Nature.* Rev. ed. N.Y., W. W. Norton & Co., 1929.

——, ——. *The Quest for Certainty.* N.Y., Minton Balch & Co., 1929.

——, ——. "Conduct and Experience" in *Psychologies of 1930.* Mass., Clark University Press, 1930.

——, ——. *How We Think.* Rev. ed. N.Y., D.C. Heath & Co., 1933.

——, ——. *Art As Experience.* N.Y., Minton Balch & Co., 1934.

——, ——. *Logic: The Theory of Inquiry.* N.Y., Henry Holt & Co., 1938.

——, ——. *Problems of Men.* N.Y., Philosophical Library, 1946.

Dewey, John and Bently, Arthur F. "Interaction and Transaction." *The Journal of Philosophy* XLIII, 19:505-517, September 1946.

220

Dewey, John. "Common Sense and Science: Their Respective Frames of Reference." *The Journal of Philosophy* XLV, 8:197-208, April 1948.

Hook, Sidney. *John Dewey* an Intellectual Portrait. N.Y., The John Day Co., 1939.

Nagel, Ernest. "Some Leading Principles of Professor Dewey's Logical Theory" in "A Symposium of Reviews of John Dewey's *Logic: The Theory of Inquiry*," *The Journal of Philosophy* XXXVI, 21:576-581, October 1939.

Ratner, Joseph, ed. *Intelligence in the Modern World*. John Dewey's Philosophy. N.Y., The Modern Library, 1939.

Russell Bertrand. *The ABC of Relativity*. N.Y., Harper & Bros, 1925.

————, ————. *Philosophy*. N.Y., W. W. Norton & Co., 1927.

————, ————. *An Inquiry into Meaning and Truth*. N.Y., W.W. Norton & Co., 1940.

Santayana, George. "Dewey's Naturalistic Metaphysics." *The Journal of Philosophy* XXII, 25:673-688, December 1925.

2.

SUPPLEMENTARY SOURCES

Cohen, Morris R. "John Dewey" In *A Preface to Logic*. N.Y., Holt & Co., 1944.

Costello, H. T. "Hypotheses and Instrumental Logicians." *The Journal of Philosophy* XV, 3:57-64, January 1918.

————, ————. "Professor Dewey's Judgments of Practise." *The Journal of Philosophy* XVII, 17:449-455, August 1920.

Dewey, John. "Reality as Experience." *The Journal of Philosophy*, III, 10:253-257, May 1906.

————, ————. *The Influence of Darwin on Philosophy and Other Essays in Contemporary Thought*. N.Y., Henry Holt and Co., 1910.

————, ————. *Essays in Experimental Logic*. Chicago, The University of Chicago Press, 1916.

————, ————. "The Development of American Pragmatism" In *Studies in the History of Ideas*. Vol. II. N.Y., Columbia University Press, 1925.

———, ———. "The Applicability of Logic to Existence. " *The Journal of Philosophy* XXVII, 27:174-1779, March 1930.

———, ———. *Philosophy and Civilization*. N.Y., Minton, Balch & Co., 1931.

Hook, Sidney. ed. *John Dewey: Philosopher of Science & Freedom*. A Symposium. N. Y., The Dial Press, 1950.

Lewis, C. I. "Meaning and Action" In "A Symposium of Reviews of John Dewey's *Logic: The Theory of Inquiry*." *The Journal of Philosophy* XXXVI, 21:572-576, October 1939.

Nagel, Ernest. "Dewey's Reconstruction of Logical Theory." *The Philosopher of the Common Man*. N.Y., G. P. Putnam's Sons, 1940.

Schilpp, Paul Arthur, ed. *The Philosophy of John Dewey*. The Library of Living Philosophers Vol. I. Evanston and Chicago, Northwestern University, 1939.

Woodbridge, Frederick, J. E. "Experience and Dialectic." *The Journal of Philosophy* XXVII, 10:264-271, May 1930.